FOURTH-GENERATION

CORPORATE SECURITY

ASYMMETRICAL WARFARE FOR PROTECTIVE SERVICES
PROFESSIONALS

R.J. GODLEWSKI

Fourth-Generation Corporate Security: Asymmetrical Warfare for Protective Services Professionals

Create Space Independent Publishing Platform

ISBN: 1490994815
ISBN-13: 978-1490994819

TABLE OF CONTENTS

DEDICATION

To all who devote his or her life to defeating evil, wherever it may be found, and protecting innocent human lives wherever they may live.

ACKNOWLEDGMENTS

To God the Father, the Son, and the Holy Spirit, without Whom I would find no talent, no opportunity, and no friends with which to affect either my trade or my interests.

Deo gratias.

4GW: AN INTRODUCTION

Fourth-Generation Warfare (4GW) represents conflict simultaneously engaged within martial, religious, political, and economic theaters.[1] Often, though not exclusively, such conflict represents an asymmetrical environment in which one party offsets limitations through concentration on another's weaknesses. For instance, Islamic jihadists may seek to target the much larger and more powerful United States through the media, understanding that the American public may shy away from open conflict against a non-state enemy. In this regard, the jihadists may attempt to wage "lawfare" – the use of the American legal system against the United States, preferring to tie up Washington in court battles regarding perceived injustices rather than confront the U.S. military directly on the battlefield.

Furthermore, by "simultaneous engagement", we do not necessarily mean that al-Qaeda, Hezbollah, drug trafficking organizations (DTO) and other "non-state" combatants function within the four 4GW elements concurrently; they may, for example, shift to economic disturbances while shoring military capabilities. Alternatively, they may

---

[1] As with all studies of human behavior, many professionals and academics question the validity of categorizing war into specific generations. See, for instance, David S. Sorenson, "The mythology of fourth-generation warfare: a response to Hammes" in *Global Insurgency and the Future of Armed Conflict: Debating Fourth-Generation Warfare* eds. Terry Terriff, Aaron Karp, and Regina Karp (New York: Routledge, 2008), 95-100. Regardless, this text keeps traditional 4GW classifications intact for convenience.

elect to concentrate on pushing religious and political influence if they cannot target economic interests directly. Nevertheless, 4GW requires that the asymmetrical participant fully engage within these core foundations while they strive for his or her objective. In this manner, 4GW becomes an entire way of life for the practitioner, more so than, perhaps, any other form of societal conflict.

4GW thus resembles a poker game rather than a chess match, each side banking upon his or her ability to read the other's mind than adhering to a much more rigid game of rules and protocol. A pertinent example of this remains the 1999 "Battle of Seattle" that pit World Trade Organization (WTO) protesters, Black Bloc anarchists, labor unions, and municipal law enforcement agencies against one another.[2] For its role, the Direct Action Network (DAN) fielded a few small units of activists to "shut down" the WTO conference.[3] Labor, in the guise of the AFL-CIO, preferred to stage a march towards downtown from a rally held at the Seattle Center.[4] The presence of the WTO and a labor rally was certainly on the minds of the Seattle police department. Unfortunately, the police wrongfully assumed that a peaceful labor rights march would draw in disaffected protestors and the combined group could be channeled along the authorized parade route. Instead, Black Bloc anarchists took advantage of the situation and accepted every opportunity to vandalize retail shops and offices under the cover provided by the more peaceful marchers.[5]

The fall 1999 fiasco in Seattle illustrates the difficulties in combating 4GW for the uninitiated. The Seattle police leadership simply concluded that they could utilize one group of unsatisfied individuals to corral another. What turned out to be the case, however, was that relatively few groups of decentralized anarchists were able to disrupt an entire city as they mingled with both the WTO protestors and the labor union marchers. A similar occurrence took place in Los Angeles when elements of the Salvadoran street gang *Mara Salvatrucha* (MS-13) capitalized upon civic unrest following the acquittal of four police officers accused of beating Rodney King to fuel an urban riot. A portion of the rationale for creating such a disturbance can, arguably, be made for disrupting ongoing trials of narcotraffickers that had been in process during late 1992/early 1993 in Washington. However, some researchers attribute this deceptive practice

---

[2] Paul de Armond, "Netwar in the Emerald City: WTO Protest Strategy and Tactics" in *Networks and Netwars" The Future of Terror, Crime, and Militancy* eds. John Arquilla and David Ronfeldt (Santa Monica, CA: RAND Corporation, 2001), 201-235.
[3] Ibid., 204.
[4] Ibid., 209.

to other guerrilla and insurgent groups, most notably Islamist radicals.[6]

Semantics aside, what 4GW implies is a universal approach to waging conflict, shattering the boundaries of "innocent parties" (political and economic warfare affects everyone, despite his or her role in active hostilities). It involves a decentralized field of battle without proximal front lines. For practitioners of security and protective services, the demarcation lines remain even more apparitional:

Table 1. Comparisons of generational conflicts for military and security disciplines.

Category	Military	Security
First-Generation	Tactics of line and column, incorporating smoothbore muskets and well-orchestrated marches against symmetrical adversaries.	Reliance upon state-funded apparatuses for prevention and response.
Second-Generation	Tactics of attacking concentrations of enemy soldiers.	Reliance upon industry standards and certifications for acceptance.
Third-Generation	Tactics of bypassing enemy strengths to target strategic assets in order to reduce casualties.	Shift toward Information Technology (IT) specific policies to safeguard assets in lieu of physical security.
Fourth-Generation	Simultaneous battle in martial, religious, economic, and political arenas.	All-inclusive, _lifestyle_ approach towards security applications.

[5] Ibid., 220.
[6] H. John Poole, *Militant Tricks: Battlefield Ruses of the Islamic Insurgent* (Emerald Isle, NC: Posterity Press, 2005), 191,

Many – if not most – security companies remain within concepts of second-generation warfare (2GW), preferring to acquiesce to expectations of antiquated methods of 'industry certification'. Others, attempting to emulate the third generation (3GW), erroneously assume that information security (IS or InfoSec) remains the *sole* requirement, as if protecting computers and data above *people* warrants consideration. Unfortunately, these companies remain at the mercy of 4GW belligerents who more effectively manage their assets. The final group, adherents of a "fourth-generation" mentality, understands the fundamental requirements of the modern world, where borders and civility disappear.

Largely reared in areas of eternal violence, such as the Middle East and Northern Africa (MENA), these practitioners adopt a stronger, warrior approach to security, acknowledging the need to defend against threats from any quarter and employing any weapon.[7] These visionaries (actually, pragmatists) effectively combine 4GW with corporate security, leading to a more militant (if not *militarized*) notion of protective services. From here, the concept of Fourth-Generation Corporate Security (4GCS) can be formulated:

The concept of merging martial, religious, economic, and political aspects of society into methods and doctrine for defending innocent human life and commercial operations from harm and disruption.

Accepting this definition – rather, like so many aspects of 4GW itself, a presumed inspiration taken from this simple definition – practitioners can begin to shed those more archaic aspects of earlier security practices ineffective for a rapidly disintegrating world. That is, 4GCS cannot be handled through shift-work, employ temporary workers, or accept transients without degradation of effectiveness. Terrorists, transnational criminal elements, and even "lone wolf" psychopaths do *not* possess an "off" button. Neither should protective services personnel.

The vast majority of asymmetrical threats targeting modern security operations hail from the same culture that permitted Saint Simeon Stylites (390?-459 A.D.) to live "uninterruptedly" for thirty years perched atop a sixty-foot pillar no larger than the average office chair.[8] These individuals are not weakened by an excessive reliance upon technology nor do they consider the time or date. For those belligerents reared within the

---

[7] Garret Machine, *Israeli Security Warrior Training* (Boulder: Paladin Press), 7.
[8] Will Durant, The Age of Faith (New York: Simon and Schuster, 1950), 60.

Middle East, their aggression literally hails from the days of Ishmael and Isaac.[9] For those not familiar with succession through birth order, the modern Palestinian-Israeli conflict may appear sophomoric and, therefore, lead them to imagine that any number of modern political solutions might remain valid. Modern political experimentation, however, cannot override centuries' worth of tribal, Bedouin practices and tradition. One cannot alter bloodline with simple sound bites.

The first rule of security remains, always, to deal with the cultures one is dealt. No matter how "enlightened" an individual may consider him or herself, for instance, employing women in roles of leadership within the Middle East is probably not a good idea. There may be exceptions – such as using women to protect women – but the standard remains to adjust one to the local traditions and expectations. This rule appears ignored by the United States, but private security firms do not possess the raw power or influence of transient American politics. Of course, being culturally aware does not absolve one of remaining ethical in practice (see next chapter). Rather, the practitioner of corporate security must always address the core values of the business providing such services. Obviously, one company may feel more comfortable dealing with certain traditions than another may. For instance, a Christian-centric company may feel more comfortable dealing with Jewish patrons than, perhaps, a secularized business would feel dealing with an overtly Islamist organization.

From a purely mathematical consideration, the 4GCS equation rests as:

Military Awareness + Religious Consideration + Political Savvy + Economic Influence = Security

Remove or lighten either of these elements and security begins to disrupt. Threats, however, simply need to tweak only one element before an imbalance begins to drop the level of security.

At its most basic level, corporate security thus requires four times the effort of a threatening individual or group. Confronting protective services personnel include guerrillas and insurgents that reign heavily in

---

[9] The present Arab-Israeli conflict can be attributed to succession rights regarding Abraham's firstborn son, Ishmael (conceived through slave Hagar), and his second born Isaac (conceived through wife Sarah) and representing Arabs and Jews respectively. See Anthony M. Davis, *Terrorism and the Maritime Transportation System: Are We on a Collision Course?*(Livermore, CA: WingSpan Press, 2008), 16-17.

the military perspective, Islamic jihadists and their supporters that misuse American religious freedoms, "civil liberties" groups as such the ACLU that burden court schedules, and Occupy Wall Street types that seek to intensify class warfare. Of course, all four groups cross 4GCS lines – which represents the crux of the discussion – but each favors a particular segment of the equation. Where 4GW threats excel over corporate security is that the former understands that perception remains an active discipline.[10] Ordinary individuals see it as a passive attribute – one "automatically" considered by the five senses.[11]

Security professionals must strive to overcome mirror imaging – the process by which one inputs his or her own expectations upon another individual or situation – which, itself, owes much to the "extraordinary extent to which the information obtained by an observer depends upon the observer's own assumptions and preconceptions."[12] In other words, what one sees is what one *expects* to see. A worst case scenario of this is exemplified by the 1932 U.S. Army-Navy war game in which the operation's umpires ruled that the victorious Navy sidestepped the laws of war – it being improper to begin a war on Sunday!"[13] Because 4GW bides by no dates or schedules, to assume that a "lifestyle war" cannot begin on a Sunday remains ludicrous. As does the notion that the earth's six billion inhabitants who could care less about Sunday view the day with any degree of admiration or respect.

Consider the following examples of 4GW participants shattering conventional expectations:

1. *La Familia Michoacana* members tossing five human heads onto a nightclub floor in Uruapan, Michoacán. Mexico on September 6, 2006 declaring "divine justice" for those whom the group felt "deserved to die";[14]

2. The Palestinian teenager who boasted on television about his propensity to plunge his axe and knife into victims after he had "tortured them for days with bare electrical wires, gouged out their eyes, cut off their tongues, and castrated them" before "slicing and

---

[10] Richards J. Heuer, Jr. *Psychology of Intelligence Analysis* (Washington: Central Intelligence Agency/Center for the Study of Intelligence, 1999), 7.
[11] Ibid.
[12] Ibid.
[13] Andrew F. Krepinevich, *7 Deadly Scenarios: A Military Futurist Explores War in the Twenty-First Century* (New York: Bantam Books, 2010), 3.
[14] George W. Grayson, *La Familia Drug Cartel: Implications for U.S.-Mexican Security* (Carlisle, PA: Strategic Studies Institute, December 2010), 1.

chopping up his victims;"[15]

3. *Los Zetas* – the now undisputed king of narco-trafficking security forces – borne of 31 deserters from Mexican special forces who excel in "rapid deployment, aerial assaults, marksmanship, ambushes, intelligence collection, counter-surveillance techniques, prisoner rescues, sophisticated communications, and the art of intimidation";[16]

4. Aum Shinrikyo – perpetrators of the notorious Tokyo subway Sarin gas attacks in 1995 – possessed 30,000 followers in Russia alone, many of which were drawn from former Soviet weapons programs and the cult itself provided services to numerous international governmental agencies;[17]

5. Followers of Bhagwan Shree Rajneesh, an Indian guru, poisoned 751 patrons of ten Oregon restaurants with salmonella in 1984 in an attempt to sway local elections;[18]

6. The Sea Tigers – naval unit of the terroristic Liberation Tigers of Tamil Eelam (LTTE) – kept Sri Lankan military and government forces at bay with a sophisticated maritime unit consisting of fast attack craft, mother ships, and deep sea weapons logistics programs;[19]

7. Narcotics trafficking organizations have developed self-propelled, semisubmersible (SPSS) and self-propelled, fully submersible (SPFS) vessels along with advanced underwater robotic devices to transport cocaine, personnel, and other contraband by the tons to American waters.

All of these groups, to varying extent, have employed asymmetrical advantage to develop expertise in that particular organization's 4GW segment. The implications for security providers remains extraordinary as no current companies can boast of, say, a true navy or provide the lethality expressed by these criminal groups.

---

[15] Eugene Sockut, *Secrets of Street Survival – Israeli Style: Staying Alive in a Civilian War Zone* (Boulder: Paladin Press, 1995), 98.

[16] Hal Brands, *Mexico's Narco-Insurgency and U.S. Counterdrug Policy* (Carlisle, PA: Strategic Studies Institute, May 2009), 8.

[17] Jonathan B. Tucker, *War of Nerves: Chemical Warfare from World War I to Al-Qaeda* (New York: Pantheon Books, 2006), 341.

[18] John R. Vacca, *Computer Forensics: Computer Crime Scene Investigation* (Hingham, MA: Charles River Media, 2002), 343.

[19] Paul A. Povlock, "A Guerilla War At Sea: The Sri Lankan Civil War", *Small Wars Journal* (September 9, 2011).

These security shortcomings are rather cultural than philosophical, as most businesses that provide security solutions often view their business as akin to, or subordinate of, law enforcement agencies.[20] To the contrary, security and law enforcement – whether federal, state, or municipal – remain diametrically opposed to one another. Police agencies, by common definition, are designed and staffed to arrive at the scene *after* a crime has been committed. Security groups response to active and *potential* threats while doing everything possible to stop aggression and penetration of their area of control. More importantly, in consideration of many recent shootings within the United States, the public no longer values police units massing outside the crisis zone; they want one or two brave officers to do what they are paid to do – enter the facility and take down the shooter.[21]

If public citizens expect their taxpayer-funded services to risk life and limb to protect them, then companies and organizations paying for professional security services can be expected to demand even *more* from their protective services contractor. In this regard, such providers must adhere to stringent levels of ethical behavior, intelligence gathering, martial power, religious devotion, political insight, and economic prowess. Consideration will now shift to their individually in appreciation of 4GCS objectives and limitations.

---

[20] Russell L. Colling and Tony W. York, *Hospital and Healthcare Security* (Oxford: Elsevier, 2010), 159-179.
[21] H. John Poole, *Tequila Junction: 4th-Generation Counterinsurgency* (Emerald Isle, Posterity Press, 2008), 182.

ETHICS

Author and veteran U.S. Navy SEAL (Sea, Air, Land) Dick Couch discusses the "moral compass" that distinguishes American soldiers from other countries' conscripts.[22] More profoundly, perhaps, Couch compares the guilt to do only good felt by devout Roman Catholics tempted with sinful behavior with the guilt experienced by U.S. Marines fearing the tarnishing of the overall Corps' image.[23] This combined philosophy is not without value to the security profession and, therefore, should serve as the foundation for practitioners of 4GCS. For the most part, however, we shall simply contend ourselves with the 2,000+ year moral authority of the Catholic Church as it applies to self-defense and protection of individuals.

In view of the protective services industry, several aspects of the *Catechism of the Catholic Church* shall be quoted for discussion:[24]

   ✓ **#2263**: "The legitimate defense of persons and societies is not an exception to the prohibition against the murder of the innocent that constitutes intentional killing. 'The act of self-defense can have a double effect: the preservation of one's own life; and the killing of the aggressor...The one is intended, the other is not.'"

---

[22] Dick Couch, *A Tactical Ethic: Moral Conduct in the Insurgent Battlespace* (Annapolis, MD: Naval Institute Press, 2010), 14.
[23] Ibid., 95.
[24] United States Catholic Conference, Inc., *Catechism of the Catholic Church* (New York: Doubleday, 1994). [Numbers in brackets indicate paragraphs of the *CCC*].

✓ **#2264**: "Love toward oneself remains a fundamental principle of morality. Therefore it is legitimate to insist on respect for one's own right to life. Someone who defends his life is not guilty of murder even if he is forced to deal his aggressor a lethal blow:...Nor is it necessary for salvation that a man omit the act of *moderate self-defense* [emphasis added] to avoid killing the other man, *since one is bound to take more care of one's own life than of another's* [emphasis added]."

✓ **#2265**: Legitimate defense can be not only a right but a *grave duty* [emphasis added] for someone responsible for another's life, the common good of the family or of the state."

✓ **#2266**: "Preserving the common good of society requires rendering the aggressor *unable to inflict harm* [emphasis added]..."

From these four snippets, a foundation of ethical defense emerges. First, self-defense – even *lethal force* – is not a prohibited action if taken in moderation. Second, individuals remain duly bound to take care of their own life first but also bear a "grave duty" to protect those under their care. Finally, the "common good of society" requires rendering aggressors impotent.

Private security businesses – arguably predating state-funded services – have always maintained "...individuals have a perfect right to protect themselves, or to hire people to protect them and their property" in the words of authors Christopher Dobson and Ronald Payne.[25] Hiring others to protect you simply remains a case of extended *self*-defense. In Western democracies, the "state" simply represents *one option* in the provision of personal and property protection. In reality, the *only* way that a state can provide adequate services is if every man, woman, and child bore his or her own protector. Obviously, this leads to a police state beyond an Orwellian scale. Accordingly, personal protection becomes a "grave duty" on a massive scale, one that only private enterprise can hope to service. Yet, what are the limits of such private protection? Frankly, very little.

Private Security Companies (PSC) assisting or contracting in Iraq following the Operation Iraqi Freedom invasion by the United States

---

[25] Christopher Dobson and Ronald Payne, *COUNTERATTACK: The West's Battle Against the Terrorists* (New York: Facts on File, 1982), 164.

gained notoriety – and much bad press – for the impression that they remained quick to shoot at any Iraqi citizen moving.[26] Nevertheless, the publicized problems in post-invasion Iraq can be attributed to the extraordinary wealth generated during *any* "gold rush" period. The rapid and massive influx of individuals – many, if not most, of whom bore no intention of serving within the field prior to the marketing of riches to be made – skew objective analysis of any opportunity. Couch discusses this as the "pirate factor" – a few disreputable individuals that destroy the integrity of a group as a whole by pirating the morality of future participants.[27]

The realization of 4GCS mandates consideration of this extremity. That is, if 4GCS remains a 'lifestyle' approach to security, then the brash and the ignorant are ultimately weeded out through attrition (economic failure), casualty, or dismissal. Practicing 4GCS cannot be a 'get rich quick' scheme for the return on 40, 50, even 100 years does not justify the effort based upon anticipated income alone. To be considered worthwhile, the practitioner *must* evaluate his or her involvement on a plane not considered by traditional providers of security. In the view of the *Catechism* on moderating free market capitalism: "Reasonable regulation of the marketplace and economic initiatives, in keeping with a just hierarchy of values and a view to the common good, is to be commended."[28]

Therefore, as unbridled capitalism remains as disruptive as omnipotent government, the practitioner of 4GCS must balance the twin issues of "economic initiative" and "hierarchal values". One must fully balance "the common good of society" with the expectation that such society rarely does anything good on its own. Such considerations flow through Michael L. Gross's theorized two-stage distillation model, the author writing, "Given free rein, there is probably no end to a person's capacity to envision new and interesting ways to disable an enemy."[29] Herein we find exceptional value in 4GCS – the *individual*, if given such free reign, remains able to envision new tactics and procedures and develop such innovations faster than would bureaucratic organizations.

Security falls into that gray area between actual military operations, where soldiers are largely permitted to kill enemy combatants

---

[26] Robert Young Pelton, *Licensed to Kill: Hired Guns in the War on Terror* (New York: Three Rivers Press, 2007), 337-339.
[27] Couch, *Tactical Ethic*, 5.
[28] *Catechism*, #2425.

with little regulation, and law enforcement activities where police officers remain far more circumscribed.[30] On the one hand, war remains the desire to force an enemy to do one's will through the maximum application of force to disarm said enemy.[31] The (thus far) four generations of warfare simply remain a tool to describe the cyclic nature of "inventing a better mousetrap" to gain strategic advantage over an adversary when, in fact, 4GW really represents the foundation for all primal conflicts. The other, law enforcement, hand represents the consideration of the socialization process of ethical behavior – "...the study of right and wrong, duty, responsibility, and personal character" that flows from the dominant system of belief orchestrated by the parent organization; in this case, the municipal, state, and federal law enforcement community.[32]

Here we have the combined intent and urge to kill with the desire to protect, serve, and apprehend that forms the basis for all security operations. More importantly, as private security and protective services constitute a legitimate business operation (i.e., one usually engaged within for profit), a balance must be struck between maximum return and the morals of society and the individuals that constitute such society.[33] In this regard, "ethics" is determined by the policies, training, and procedures required of employees and incorporating those individuals' base culture.[34] Naturally, security personnel running around shooting individuals at random would draw the ire of both indigenous military and law enforcement agencies, but *when* would protective services personnel be *expected* to return fire? To answer that question, we must retreat a bit and discuss what the security environment within 4GW entails.

Any functioning protection program involves the "three pillars" of security: people, processes, and physical safeguards.[35] Effective security operations must consider these elements and analyze how they mesh with

---

[29] Michael L. Gross, *Moral Dilemmas of Modern War: Torture, Assassination, and Blackmail in an Age of Asymmetric Conflict* (New York: Cambridge University Press, 2010), 241-242.

[30] Ibid., 103-104.

[31] Carl von Clausewitz, *On War* ed. and trans. Michael Howard and Peter Paret (Princeton, NJ: Princeton University Press, 1976), 75-77.

[32] Quote in Stan Stojkovic, David Kalinich, and John Klofas, *Criminal Justice Organizations: Administration and Management, Fifth Edition* (Belmont, CA: Wadsworth, 2012), 277.

[33] Philip P. Purpura, *Security and Loss Prevention: An Introduction, Fifth Edition* (Burlington, MA: Elsevier, 2008), 39.

[34] Ibid., 40.

[35] John J. Fay, *Contemporary Security Management, Third Edition* (Burlington, MA: Elsevier, 2011), 412-413.

the actions of adversarial forces.

- **People**: Transnational criminal organizations (TCO), whether consisting of Islamic jihadists or narcotics traffickers, represent diverse social networks presenting a web culture of a multitude of roles, personalities, and obligations.[36] They survive through competitive adaptation to elude the capabilities of counterterrorist or counternarcotics agents as appropriate.[37] To defend against these innovative adversaries, security organizations must employ individuals that not only understand the mentality of their quarry, but can also employ "ethical adaptation" to ensure that his or her efforts remain acceptable to the surrounding culture. 4GW is, at its most fundamental level, a popularity contest between claims of *"It's a horrible idea for you to change your ways..."* and its eternal competitor *"Brother, have I got something great in store for you!"*[38] Security services must win the publicity campaign and this entails recruiting and hiring only exceptional (ethically) talent;

- **Processes**: if ineffective people can sabotage a security operation, faulty security *processes* can inflict much more damage. Part of this reality comes from the recognition that a particular company's doctrine and rules govern how such individuals function. Litigators understand that very few individuals possess sufficient wealth to warrant their interests; therefore, they will seek whatever claim they can make to place full responsibility upon the security *company* itself even if the individual consciously committed the grievance without influence. For this reason, security procedures must be detailed enough to address every conceivable situation and, yet, flexible enough to adjust operations 'on the fly';

- **Physical Security**: there remains a preference today to equate "security" with information technology (IT) and while the protection of data and other attributes of IT security remain important for the consumer and business, *physical* assets

---

[36] Michael Kenney, *From Pablo to Osama: Trafficking and Terrorist Networks, Government Bureaucracies, and Competitive Adaptation* (University Park, PA: The Pennsylvania State University Press, 2007), 26-36.
[37] Ibid., 6.
[38] R.J. Godlewski, "Latte Intelligence: The Divorce of Shock Creativity and Special Information Operations", *American Intelligence Journal* 29, no. 1 (2011): 72.

represents the *cible extraordinaire* for terrorists. This is because despite the tremendous damage that can be achieved through targeting financial assets, for example, Islamic jihadists and other political-based extremists seek to gain the notoriety of media coverage. And nothing gains this notoriety faster than images of buildings and other structures in flames (think Mumbai, India). Moreover, jihadists can achieve the moral high ground if they can produce images – and all but the smallest cells maintain video post-production capabilities – of security forces violating their rights or that of "innocent parties". Security, on the other hand, must strive to protect these physical locations without falling victim to terrorist propaganda campaigns.

With these brief thoughts in mind, security can now begin to analyze a proper 4GCS ethics policy.

Being, naturally, a human endeavor, 4GW requires a *human* solution to problems. In military circles, this generally results in some manner of counterinsurgency (COIN) operation where practitioners attempt to win the "hearts and minds" of a disaffected population. Security, however, does not represent a temporal problem, as would be the case with an invading army. On the contrary, protective services are either a community constituent or a tourist manifestation (as in the case of executive protection accompanying a VIP into a foreign location). The point at which security *must win* the hearts and minds of an indigenous population is precisely the point when it already lost the battle.

4GCS pulls in supporters because they remain afraid to join any other function. That is, aiding and supporting security efforts has to entail a public victory. How? Because superior ethics trumps superior terror and persuasion. This may not always appear to be the case, but even the most stoical individual is "naturally" drawn towards the good fight – which means that he or she receives some personal benefit from the association. Consider this example. Following the battle at Gettysburg during the American Civil War, 27,574 muskets were recovered – some 90% loaded, 12,000 of these loaded more than once, and about 6,000 loaded anywhere from three to ten, one even *twenty-three* times![39] The height of brutality – civil war – did not persuade thousands of soldiers to abandon ethical treatment of fellow human beings: they merely *pretended* to engage within conflict.

---

[39] Dave Grossman, *On Killing: The Psychological Cost of Learning to Kill in War and Society* (New York: Back Bay Books, 2009), 23.

These were conscript (i.e., "citizen") soldiers thrust into horrifying battles. Yet, highly trained special operations forces (SOF) soldiers, such as Navy SEALs and Army Green Berets, who can only volunteer for service, commonly exhibit unethical behavior.[40] This suggests that highly qualified and highly screened soldiers can still evolve into "pirates" as easily and as consciously as unsatisfactory applicants of the traditional military can. The best candidates routinely come from backgrounds that stress the primacy of family, faith, and positive role models.[41]

For this reason in particular, security services must always present the image of *protecting innocent human lives*, a very complicated endeavor within any armed conflict or social crisis. Even during natural disasters such as hurricanes and earthquakes, citizens will begin to develop a sense of hostility towards government and/or military personnel. Part of this stems, as in the case of Hurricane Katrina in New Orleans, Louisiana, from any bureaucracy's inability to deliver services and supplies as promised. This further explains why militaries spend a great deal of time conditioning soldiers to fire when and only *when* instructed to do so from authority figures.[42] The natural inclination of all humans during crises remains to fend for oneself – basic survival.

Where security services prevail rests with their ability to "hire" from within the indigenous population. This is a key component; security *must* be an indigenous effort to succeed. The affected population must be a part of the security apparatus if the protective services campaign is to remain a part of the local population. Poole expands upon this, declaring that local political organizations and processes are of the most importance to 4GW operations.[43] It must be remembered, however, that no facet of 4GW can remain dominant for any period before the equation of conflict disrupts its rhythm. Politics may corral the masses, yes, but the population is generally concerned about economics and/or religion. If politicians still desire to control their constituency outside of these parameters, than only military force will suffice – for a time.

Traditionally, security has always dealt with issues that affected a company's inner perimeter, such as disgruntled employees, a prying competitor, or, at worst, a gang of protestors hanging banners on the fence. Yet, with the possible exception of the disgruntled worker, all of these threats materialized from far away. As with 4GW threats in general, they do

---

[40] Couch, *Tactical Ethic*, 3.
[41] Ibid., 74.
[42] Grossman, *Killing.*, 262.
[43] Poole, *Tequila*, 184.

not appear from within a vacuum. On the contrary, threats evolve from the time, location, perception, and attitude of the indigenous environment affected by the political, security, or military apparatus targeted.

Figure 1. World of threats confronting 4GCS ethics. Background images, © Stasys Eidiejus -, © mixformdesign -, © ktsdesign - Fotolia.com

These threats represent a sea of hostility that washes upon the shore of the affected facility, sometimes generating a few ripples and at other times blowing in a raging gale. Nevertheless, the progenitor of these "climatic" conditions hail from nearly anywhere in the world owing to the advent of modern communications technology and the Internet. These forces ensure that any effort by the security team remains magnified exponentially for the entire viewing world to scrutinize and criticize. Ethics, therefore, remains the key to turning these tides away from the company and back out into the World Wide Web where equality of opinion bears a chance. Silence is not an attribute when others conspire in libel.

Because ethics remains such an integral part of 4GCS it, too, must encapsulate an 'all or nothing' way of life. Too often, professional services companies segregate lives. We often, for example, read of a prominent chief financial officer whose personal finances are in shambles. Alternately, we may discover the leader of a powerful organization ridiculed because his or her family disintegrates. There are other stories of a "best in the business" transportation company whose employees could not make it out of the parking lot in the afternoon without creating five or six accidents. At the beginning of this chapter, we spoke of parallels between the Catholic Church and the U.S. Marines. This analysis remains quite apropos for 4GCS must employ "the few, the proud, the *holy*."

It may not appear easy to live a life of complete ethical consideration and many individuals may, perhaps correctly, scrutinize the presence of "religious doctrine" within the security field, but such *must* be the case when dealing with human lives. Only *legitimate* public authority may provide capital justice, "not excluding in cases of extreme gravity, the death penalty."[44] Security personnel may, if rarely, take down an individual, but such must be the case of *intending* to protect another individual's life as per *CCC* #2264. That is, the subconscious rationalization of "this person's death is going to save *whose* immediate life?" should always be considered – in an ideal situation.

Whatever the context, 4GCS has to function as a higher-order social program. It may be somewhat difficult to develop a matrix for deciding shoot/no shoot scenarios, for instance, but each individual must be held to a higher authority in determining when to employ lethal force (Note: in 4GCS, the individual directly confronting the threat retains such authority in how to protect his or her life, as well as those under their direct care). Often, in war zones in particular, shooting becomes contagious; security personnel begin targeting *anything* that appears even remotely threatening. Unfortunately, even with many lives saved, the resulting backlash from the collateral damage will suffocate the entire security industry.

For this reason, ethics demands that practitioners of 4GCS employ actionable intelligence as a force-multiplier to eliminate innocent deaths. Only by intimately understanding the threat, and precisely *who* the prime movers are, can participants in 4GCS scale the situation down to the very individual that is targeting the protected entity. This aids in efficiency, too, for 4GCS devotees possess neither the luxury nor the diplomacy of nations to ignore even the slightest error in judgment. With one wrong situation or indiscriminate employee and the security company could very well become targeted itself as either an aggressor or, in extreme cases, as a bona fide terrorist organization.

Therefore, 4GCS *must* become the pantheon of ethical behavior,

---

[44] *Catechism*, #2266.

illuminating the world of international security and protective services as a beacon of chivalry, respect, and admiration by all – including potential adversaries. Ethics is, thus, the guiding star. Now, however, we must turn to the powerful engine.

ACTIONABLE INTELLIGENCE

Intelligence represents the acquisition and utilization of information that can provide a tactical and strategic advantage for the collector.[45] It remains "about reducing uncertainty in conflict."[46] Perhaps more colloquially, intelligence describes the field of gathering "a flood of genuine leaks, rumors, and bits and pieces of real significance" and building them into coherence.[47] Because intelligence benefits *any* discipline, from business to law enforcement, to the military, it should remain a common sense requirement. Unfortunately, many leaders do not attach to intelligence its proper value or utilization. For example, many managers within the correctional field do not believe in collecting intelligence regarding the prisoner population because a host of biases – both real and perceived – lead them to believe that such efforts would be useless.[48] These preconceptions regarding prisoner psychology divert them away from leaks, rumors, and bits of significance that Balor argued represented actual

---

[45] Intelligence (INT) has traditionally been segregated into derived sources, encompassing human (HUMINT), signals (SIGINT), electronic (ELINT), etc., and even, lately, Open-Source (OSINT). That said, there remains a trend to combine intelligence into 'All-Source', signifying the reality that intelligence remains beneficial if all sources are employed within an investigation.
[46] Robert M. Clark, *Intelligence Analysis: A Target-Centric Approach, Second Edition* (Washington: CQ Press, 2007), 8.
[47] Paul Balor, *Manual of the Mercenary Soldier* (Boulder: Paladin Press, 1988), 228.
[48] Stojkovic, Kalinich, and Klofas, *Criminal Justice*, 124-125

intelligence.[49]

Intelligence takes on even greater significance in combating 4GW cycles. Terrorists and other transnational groups maintain extraordinary intelligence capabilities, concentrating on the HUMINT segment for operational purposes. The Islamist group Hezbollah, for instance, had used the social networking site Facebook to gain information on individual Israeli soldiers.[50] More importantly, Hezbollah reportedly mastered counter-signals intelligence (C-SIGNET) to keep Israel from eavesdropping on its terrorist operations.[51] Such determined efforts illustrate the effectiveness of non-state groups to attack and defend against even sophisticated security agencies.

HUMINT	Human Intelligence
IMINT	Imagery Intelligence
SIGINT	Signals Intelligence
MASINT	Measurement & Signature Intelligence
ELINT	Electronics Intelligence
GEOINT	Geospatial Intelligence
OSINT	Open-source Intelligence

Table 2. Representative intelligence disciplines. Relative "types" of intelligence include political, military, scientific, technical, economic, and sociological.

Figure 2. Intelligence Cycle.

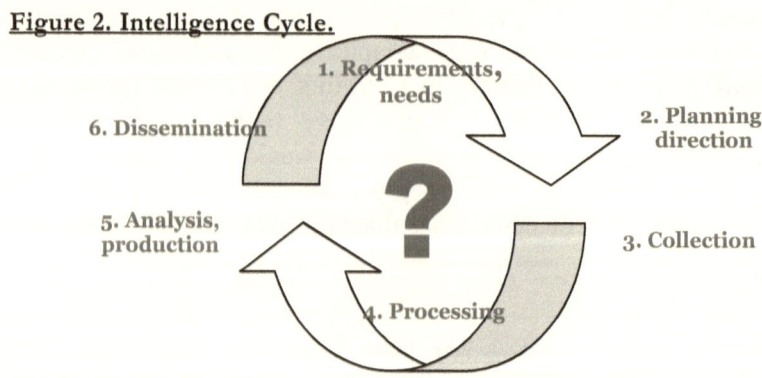

1. Requirements, needs
2. Planning, direction
3. Collection
4. Processing
5. Analysis, production
6. Dissemination

---

[49] Balor, *Mercenary*, 228-229.
[50] Graham H. Turbiville, Jr. *Guerrilla Counterintelligence: Insurgent Approaches to Neutralizing Adversary Intelligence Operations* (Hurlburt Field, FL: Joint Special Operations University, January 2009), 60.
[51] Ibid.

In 4GCS operations, intelligence collection as an offensive measure, and counterintelligence (CI) as both an active and passive defensive operation, remain critical for corporate security. In the former, providers of security must exercise every option available in order to gain actionable intelligence regarding threats and hostile groups. In the latter, security personnel must engage in deception and denial programs to keep corporate spies, terrorists, and other disgruntled persons from gaining information about the company and its operations. A large measure of both disciplines comes from the local population.

Because terrorists and other transnational criminal entities represent networked organizations, they do not need to protect physical locations as much as do nation-states and security institutions. That is, they must protect few office buildings, retail establishments, or even equipment on a daily basis. Since their organizational structures are largely apparitional, so, too, are their intelligence apparatuses. The secrecy inherent within trafficking organizations, for example, dictates that each particular "cell" operate within a compartmentalized function, sharing information with other cells solely on a need-to-know basis.[52] The hunt for Miguel and Gilberto Rodríguez-Orejuela in Colombia resulted from intelligence obtained from key informants, whom the brothers were never able to flush out.[53] Subsequent criminal groups have learned from this lesson, making informants less available, especially for private security operations.

Criminal organizations utilize what Balor refers to as *Mousseblin* – "civilian street people, rabble, and their rural counterparts" – to affect their mission.[54] These individuals are ordinarily grouped into neighborhood "blocks" and each records the arrival and departure of vehicles by license plate number and color, domestic disputes between spouses and neighbors, who returns home later than normal, and, of course, the presence of any suspicious characters.[55] Executive protection professionals (EPP) fill a similar need through a slightly different approach. When arriving within a foreign (though not necessarily international) location, they plan for their principal's arrival by obtaining as much information as possible from hotel clerks and staff and nearby retail establishments.[56]

---

[52] Kenney, *Pablo to Osama,* 27.
[53] Ibid, 105.
[54] Balor, *Mercenary*, 238.
[55] Ibid., 241.
[56] Philip T. Holder and Donna Lea Hawley, *The Executive Protection Professional's Manual* (Boston: Butterworth-Heinemann, 1998), 51.

When placing a VIP within any housing establishment, EPP teams must scrutinize every nook and cranny to determine from whence any threat may arise, but also to formulate possible avenues of egress in the event of an emergency.[57]

This is only appropriate, for *anyone* seeking to target a prominent business or political leader remains likely to have scoured all hotels within their native territory to bribe and coerce workers for just such eventualities. One could only hypothesize about the implications of the U.S. Secret Service team hiring (and using) prostitutes in Colombia during advance planning.[58] Terrorist organizations, such as al-Qaeda, Hezbollah, Hamas, etc. routinely use such "citizen-based" surveillance techniques.

KEY: 1. Convenience store. 2. Hotel. 3. Small office building. 4. Theater. 5. Retail shop. 6. Used car lot. 7. Parking garage.

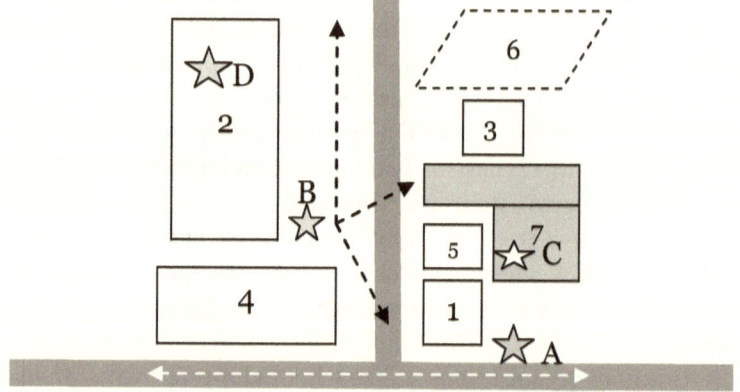

Figure 3. Schematic of criminal/terrorist surveillance network.

In the above illustration, we can see a very basic surveillance structure for a criminal network. Individual "A", possibly representing a utility worker, scrutinizes all traffic along the main highway. Individual "B" may be a hotel concierge, keeping records of all visitors to the hotel as well as identifying all vehicles entering the parking garage across the street and arriving from the side road. Informant "C" may be a parking lot attendant or simply a valet from the hotel. His or her duties would be to signal the departure of any vehicles from the garage. Individual "D" would represent

---

[57] Ibld.

virtually any of the hotel staff whose job would be to identify which visitors stay in which room, their habits, and arrival and departure schedules.

Westerners in general and Americans in particular, fail to grasp the significance of scenarios as that outlined above. This remains because our culture does not present any threat where we do not immediately find our lives in peril. This is because Americans do not understand the concept of "spying" upon one another in a nation of perceived privacy rights. Effective security professionals, to the contrary, understand the four methods of convincing another individual to turn his or her loyalty: suggest cooperation to obtain a mutual goal, bargain an exchange, fraud, and force.[59] All four find their use in any society, but let us examine how they could be utilized within, say, the United States where employer/public loyalty remains expected.

- *Mutuality*. Protective services personnel often share information with other professionals, as well as key managers of hotels, resorts, etc. House cleaners, desk clerks, janitors, even other occupants often help aid security personnel when they *believe* they are actually helping authoritative efforts. Naturally, with advanced technology and 'imagery', nearly *anyone* can masquerade as one of the 'good guys'.

- *Exchange*. Islamic jihadists and transnational criminal elements often cooperate on matters of operation. For instance, the jihadists may provide another political terrorist group with key information on how to manufacture explosive devices for use against the second group's government. Supporters of the political terrorists may, therefore, be obligated to provide actionable intelligence in return, even though the Islamists may be targeting what the political group considers as "innocent parties". Some of this information exchange takes place through, and largely because of, alternate reality sites such as Second Life where the role-playing public inadvertently provides much of the information and money-laundering opportunities.[60]

---

[58] See, for instance, http://www.foxnews.com/world/2012/04/15/obama-expect-rigorous-review-service-secret/ Accessed January 2014.
[59] Jefferson Mack, *Running a Ring of Spies: Spycraft and Black Operations in the Real World of Espionage* (Boulder: Paladin Press, 1996), 35.
[60] Steven Nutt and Josh Lyons, "Virtual Worlds and Terrorist Attack Planning," Urban Warfare Analysis Center, August 22, 2008, 1-9.

- *Fraud.* Simply another facet of deception, fraud remains a powerful tool of intelligence organizations whether they represent legitimate groups or freelancers. An intelligence operative may pose as an environmental inspector, inquiring of neighborhood conditions. Alternatively, he or she may pose as a defense investigator, seeking "pre-employment" information about a neighbor or coworker. People in the West are quite liberal with their information sharing and all that it takes is a brief deception before they become enamored with the prospect of "benefiting" a friend, family member, or close neighbor.

- *Force.* If Dr. Stanley Milgram of Yale University proved in the 1960s that 65% of the human population could be induced into rendering lethal force upon another innocent party with mere prompting from an authority figure bearing little more than a lab coat and clipboard, a greater percentage must be susceptible to coercion and blackmail for the purposes of obtaining information.[61] The threat of bodily harm to oneself remains a powerful motivator to do as the aggressor wishes. The threat of job loss, financial ruin, or even the opposite, promises of promotion and/or capital gain work wonders in getting people to loosen up with information. History is full of people who betrayed his or her country for few pittances.

The multitude of methods in which to 'turn' a particular individual simply underscores the reality that *anyone* – including long-term employees – remains under suspicion.

Again, this flies in the face of Western courtesy, the notion that *all* individuals must be treated as suspect *even after a corporation or business has vetted them*. Sadly, reality is not very conductive to feelings. Couch reiterates that even one or two bad apples within an otherwise exceptional organization can disease the entire institution as if a plague.[62] To insulate against this problem, a "no tolerance" rule must be enforced.[63] What this means is that under no circumstances must your organization accept the behavior of any individual who deviates from policy. Incidentally, such policy must be included within the employee (and contractor's) handbook and, naturally, discretion serves to prevent the terminated individual from actually becoming intelligence fodder for adversaries.

---

[61] Grossman, *On Killing*, 141.
[62] Couch, *Tactical Ethic*, 106-107.
[63] Ibid.

The never-ending cycle of intelligence gathering begins at the outermost sphere, which represents the entire planet and includes every imaginable threat to the company from the street, the air, and even outer space in the context of communications satellites and ground-imaging spacecraft. Here is where awareness remains a bit more intuitional than deeper into the company's security perimeter. Anyone can be threatening so everyone is expected. Nevertheless, few actually constitute viable threats so their presence remains anticipated more than scrutinized. Any 4GCS intelligence operation within this sphere deals exclusively with the inherent knowledge, inquisitiveness, and rational thought of the security team. Whether or not any potential threat is discovered rests exclusively with his or her ability to wade through the endless sea of clutter and isolate what remains possible if not probable.

The second, denser sphere deals with the corporate community. That is, the particular environment any operation or facility interacts with on a daily basis. This represents the final 'envelope' that individuals and mechanisms have to invade before they even begin to target your particular facility. This environment could represent a city block for a small mom-and-pop retailer or an entire country for the domestic operations of an international conglomerate. Penetration of this sphere means that potential threats no longer need to disrupt the indigenous culture before they can affect your company's operations. For example, the September 11, 2001 (9/11) hijackers answered the question, "How could nineteen young Arab men fool the CIA?"[64] What Arab academia failed to consider was that the 19 hijackers did not necessarily "fool" anyone – particularly our national security infrastructure – because America *welcomed* them in with contriteness of heart.[65] Today, security cannot be as accommodating – no matter how many sensibilities it squashes.

The final sphere represents the "red line", where trespassers bear an actionable threat for the company, its personnel (including legitimate visitors), and all equipment and processes. Specifically, this represents all properties owned or controlled by the business. In other words, corporate security personnel no longer can afford to rely upon taxpayer-funded services to provide the company with advantage. With the average response time of fifteen minutes (sometimes up to 45 minutes in locations such as Detroit), an aggressor can impose a significant amount of damage prior to aid arriving. Here is where the local citizenry expects one or two

---

[64] Fawaz A. Gerges, *Journey of the Jihadist: Inside Muslim Militancy* (Orlando, FL: Harcourt, 2006), 183.
[65] Ibid.

police officers to confront active shooters within schools rather than to muster outside and await backup in the form of Special Weapons and Tactics (SWAT) teams.[66] Corporate security *must* address the same concerns. At the point where threats materialize, it remains the duty of security to deal with them.

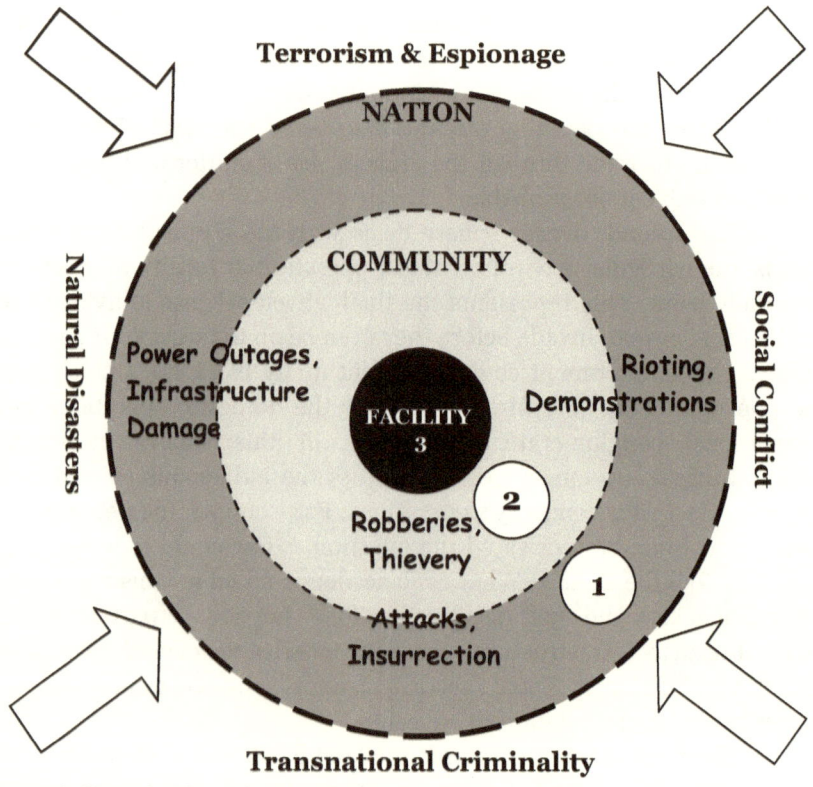

Figure 4. Security Intelligence Spheres. Condition One (Yellow Alert) represents precautionary measures and general observation. Condition Two (Orange Alert) warrants careful scrutiny and isolation of perceived threats. A Condition Three (Red Alert) represents hostile actions taken against company property, personnel, and/or operations at a specific location.

A three-phase intelligence program, such as that outlined within the above illustration, represents the most effective option for most corporate security operations. Because threats can arise from any source and during any period, Condition One (analogous to a national Yellow

---

[66] Poole, *Tequila*, 182.

Alert classification) simply means that corporate security personnel remain observant of potential natural disasters, transnational criminal activities, terrorism, and other spontaneous eruptions of social conflict. These "threats" never die out, but remain incubated under numerous conditions. Condition Two (Orange Alert) represents occurrences within a specific community that could erupt upon an individual facility or operation. Here is where international and national threats merge with local supporters or the affected population to disrupt the community where the company's offices or facilities operate.

Condition Three, or "red alert" signifies that the property under protection is under active threat, whether that represents suffering an earthquake or direct attack. At this stage, intelligence collection becomes secondary and involves more of a forensics approach. That is, active intelligence collection diverts to active protective measures and only reemerges when conditions diminish to the point where personnel can be debriefed and the aftermath photographed and cataloged for future analysis. The impetus for 4GCS rests with isolating spiraling threats from the broad sea of potentialities that masquerade as bona fide hostilities. In other words, 4GCS intelligence operations must effectively zero in on those individuals most likely to step beyond the boundaries of civility and orchestrate clear and present dangers.

As was discussed within the chapter on ethics, effective security necessitates an aggressor unable to inflict harm upon the company. This remains a double-edged sword – security must terminate the threat without itself becoming an aggressive tyrant. What this means is that security must isolate the aggressor down to the lowest denominator that will allow prudent action taken to both cease the disturbance *and permit the company to retain its good image in public*. This represents the crux of 4GCS. Nations and terrorists can target indiscriminately; security operations must become *exceptionally* discretionary in application.

Only when actionable intelligence permits the 4GCS unit to isolate a particular threat down to its *presence within an ongoing crime* can security personnel withstand the martial, religious, political, and economic implications of its actions. This requires extraordinary capability – to be *there*, fully prepared, when the terrorist or criminal decides to take a strike against the protected facility. To target individuals simply because one feels threatened leads to significant political and economic losses for the company under his or her care and this violates the tenets of traditional religious beliefs. One simply becomes a proponent of second-generation warfare (2GW), throwing massive firepower at anything and everything that moves, hoping that the bad people die in sufficient number to terminate hostilities.

Because commercial enterprises in general and security operations specifically bear limited resources and personnel, archaic "attrition" struggles remain exceptionally detrimental. This, of course, remains the purpose of international terrorists in the guise of Islamic jihadists – to turn the public against the victim. Al-Qaeda and its offshoots devote a considerable amount of time towards intelligence collection.[67] Similarly, the jihadists rank their targets in descending order of importance – from Jews to Christians (subcategorized) and, finally, apostates, declaring openly "We have come to slaughter you".[68] Being comfortable with collateral casualties, they do not mind laying grievances against their target in order to dupe others into believing that the attackers are, in fact, the "true victims".

With an effective intelligence program in place, anchored by an exceptional consideration of ethical behavior, the practitioner of 4GCS can now consider the martial aspects of his or her career. That is, 4GCS requires placing *teeth* into any protective services plan for when the time comes, he who possesses superior strength is more likely to determine what remains permissible or not.

---

[67] Norman Cigar, *Al-Qa'ida's Doctrine for Insurgency: 'Abd Al-'Aziz Al-Muqrin's A Practical Course for Guerrilla War* (Washington: Potomac Books, 2009), 122-123.
[68] Quoted in ibid., 129.

INTEGRATED TACTICAL WARFARE

War remains an intolerable subject. General William Tecumseh Sherman declared it virtual hell. The Roman Catholic Church outlines "strict conditions" for even *"legitimate defense...*subject to rigorous conditions of moral legitimacy."[69] Nevertheless, war represents a central tenet of human existence. Old Testament Scripture remains required reading for military tacticians. Clausewitz, recognizing the existence of war to force others into our will, hints at its brutality: "war is such a dangerous business that the mistakes which come from kindness are the very worst."[70] In this brief statement, the Prussian general laid down the gauntlet for practitioners of security. That is, protecting people in the 21st century remains such a "dangerous business", that security provisions based upon "kindness" do more damage than the myriad of asymmetrical threats aligned against that company or organization.

Counterterrorism expert Bruce Hoffman takes this a step further, referring to the discipline as "a nasty business".[71] To underscore this statement, Hoffman tells the story of a Sri Lankan intelligence officer convincing an LTTE terrorist into talking by flicking a few drops of gasoline into a plastic bag tightly secured around the head of the man.[72]

---

[69] *Catechism*, #2309.
[70] Clausewitz, *On War*, 75.
[71] Bruce Hoffman, "A Nasty Business" in Russell D. Howard and Reid L. Sawyer, *Terrorism and Counterterrorism: Understanding the New Security Environment: Readings and Interpretations* (Dubuque, IA: McGraw-Hill, 2006), 402-407.
[72] Ibid., 406.

Incidentally, the Sri Lankans eventually defeated the LTTE. Western sensitivities could not possibly endorse such "suffocating" techniques, but few in the West have come across an enemy that lives for killing others. Few can imagine teenagers glorifying over their ability to carve up innocent victims.[73] Such atrocities, however, are growing in occurrence rather than receding into the past. The West cannot excuse itself from this interminable reality. In fact, while Vietnam-era American soldiers were training with paper targets, their Soviet counterparts presented no such illusions, printing training manuals with depictions of their troops killing U.S. Green Beret and Airborne soldiers.[74] Practitioners of 4GCS must concentrate on defeating their enemy, not "paper" targets.

To prepare for this chapter, we have briefly discussed the prerequisites of ethics and intelligence. First, we must adhere to the moral high road, then maximize intelligence gathering to target only those individuals in the *direct process of harming innocent lives*. Now, we can conclude such stipulations with four basic assumptions:

1. Security professionals must devote his or her *entire existence* to the preservation of innocent human life, whether or not such individuals pay for protection;

2. Security professionals must acknowledge that there remain individuals within the world that will not surrender or be taken into custody; that these same individuals remain very likely to kill themselves or otherwise fight to the death before they acquiesce to legitimate authority;

3. Of the 65% of the human population proven to bear the capacity to inflict lethal force upon innocent persons, a sizeable percentage will actually mutilate, torture, and murder with little remorse;

4. Legitimate public authority, i.e., the law enforcement, political, and military institutions of a democracy, will be of little value in ceasing global aggression. For example, during the slaughter of nearly a million Rwandans, the United Nations (UN) troops sent to protect the Tutsis "offered little resistance to the killers."[75]

Practitioners of security must, therefore, accept the mentality of a warrior

---

[73] Sockut, *Street Survival*, 98.

[74] Paladin Press, *KGB Alpha Team Training Manual: How the Soviets Trained for Personal Combat, Assassination, and Subversion* (Boulder: Paladin Press, 1993), 217.

[75] Philip Gourevitch, *We wish to inform you that tomorrow we will be killed with our families: Stories from Rwanda* (New York: Picador, 1998), 114.

and consider that threats may arise from any quarter and during any period; that such a mentality acknowledges that security personnel are now engaged within a bona fide war against Islamic terrorists, narcotics traffickers, and other criminal elements that may or may not be supported by nation-states and other political organizations.[76]

Before continuing, we must address what we mean by employing the term "martial" in context of 4GW in general and its security connotations within 4GCS specifically. While the reader may correctly assume that we are discussing the attributes of warfare and conflict, the use here remains much more profound if not esoteric. The practitioner of 4GCS must develop a martial *way of life* that encompasses excellence in training, a sharpening of one's senses, and a broader approach to absorbing what the world offers.[77] As discussed more in detail within the next chapter regarding the religious elements of 4GW, the security professional, today, encounters adversaries that often come from ancient cultures where patience is determined on scales of decades at the very minimum.

If 4GCS involves the simultaneous employment of martial, religious, political, and economic aspects of life, then it can be further assumed that the lifestyle of security personnel cannot deviate from the acceptance that these four intertwined disciplines require a tremendous commitment to engage. Sadly, many aspects of American society – e.g., the MTV television programmers – apparently concluded that the 9/11 attacks were 'old news' by the first anniversary of the atrocity.[78] This despite that the attacks were a follow-up to the 1993 failure to topple the World Trade Center towers. What a large portion of the American public grew weary of within one year, Khalid Sheik Muhammad spent eight years carrying out what his nephew, Ramzi Yousef, could not do with a vehicular-borne improvised explosive device (VBIED).

The implications of this remain deafening: as soon as security personnel let their guard down, *someone* will take advantage of the situation to inflict death and destruction upon the innocent. Despite its connotation with Eastern mysticism, practitioners of 4GCS *must develop a martial way of life* if only to keep him or her on their toes. In the West, security and military applications tend to focus more on doctrine than

---

[76] Machine, *Security Warrior*, 7.

[77] Forrest E. Morgan, *Living the Martial Way: A Manual for the Way a Modern Warrior Should Think* (Fort Lee, NJ: Barricade Books, 1992), 11.

[78] Mark A. Cwiek, "America after 9/11" in eds. Gerald R. Ledlow, James A. Johnson, and Walter J. Jones, *Community Preparedness and Response to Terrorism: Volume 1: The Terrorist Threat and Community Response* (Westport, CT: Praeger, 2005), 14-14.

substance.[79] The 4GW adversaries that security personnel encounter do not endorse "doctrine" as much as they do ideology or religion. Asymmetrical threats employ what is available and not what remains expected or desired.

In this regard, security personnel cannot eliminate consideration of martial applications – defense, warfare, intensity, etc. – for the sole reason that "the other guys" will not refrain from inflicting the most horrific damage possible upon other human beings. This does *not* mean that security personnel should adopt the same measures. No sane individual blows him or herself up to promote a cause anymore than he or she beheads another to support a particular occupation. At least not within the context of benefiting society and *all* individuals making up such society. Security personnel, however, can – and *should* – employ lethal force if it remains the only means available for stopping a homicide bomber from detonating an improvised explosive device (IED) or a narco-trafficker from beheading an individual.

To paraphrase 'just war' philosophy:[80]

In order for 4GCS personnel to engage within *ethical* martial defense:

1. The damage to be inflicted by the aggressor upon the persons or properties under protection must be perceived to be lasting, grave, and certain beyond a reasonable doubt;

2. All other means of disrupting or stopping the aggressor must be judged as impractical or ineffective;

3. The security provider must determine a significant degree of success for the action to be taken;

4. The use of force must not produce circumstances (as determined by legitimate public authority, the press, or the population) that emerge as worse than that presented by the original aggressor. The power of modern technology exacerbates this consideration.

As with just war constraints, these conditions ensure that security personnel only employ force commensurate with the degree of the threat. They do not, however, diminish the need for security personnel to *prepare*

---

[79] Poole, *Tequila*, 169.
[80] *Catechism*, #2309.

for actual warfare (which, with 4GW, does not automatically imply open combat with firearms). Rather, such conditions provide 4GCS personnel with guidelines to authenticate tactical defense, which "can have a double effect: the preservation of one's one life; and the killing of the aggressor...The one is intended, the other is not."[81] To broaden the discussion of warfare, consideration of statements issued by Sun-tzu, the ancient Chinese tactician, should suffice:

> **"Warfare is the greatest affair of state, the basis of life and death, the Way [Tao] to survival or extinction. It must be thoroughly pondered and analyzed."[82]**

> **"Warfare is the Way [Tao] of deception."[83]**

> **"Thus it is said that one who knows the enemy and knows himself will not be endangered in a hundred engagements."[84]**

These statements present a solid foundation upon which to develop an effective 4GCS program. That is, the pillar of successful security rests upon realizing that one's duty is to protect under the precepts of survival or extinction; that threats to security incorporate deception as a means as well as an ends; and that tactical intelligence rests supreme.

From here, diligent analysis mandates that security evolve away from simply placing "guards" in public view. Traditionally guards have served in one of two capacities for American and Western security companies. First, they served to corral employees and visitors into expected patterns of behavior. Second, they announced to trespassers that there was "somebody" there that may, on occasion, intercept their presence. Rarely, and only in cases of defense contractors for government and/or military institutions, would guards be armed and trained to detour aggressive personnel. Even as late as the post-Cold War military draw down of the 1990s, U.S. military bases deferred to civilian security guards stationed at main gates instead of the heretofore armed Marines, soldiers, sailors, and airmen.

---

[81] *Catechism*, #2263.
[82] Ralph D. Sawyer, *The Seven Military Classics of Ancient China* (Boulder: Westview Press, 1993), 157.
[83] Ibid., 158.
[84] Ibid., 162.

Even with the advent of the 9/11 attacks in Washington and New York, security efforts still focus on corralling the public more than apprehending and subduing terrorists and transnational criminals. There remains very little public profiling of individuals to ascertain who represents a threat and who deserves to retain his or her civil liberties. Nor is there much consideration of security beyond, perhaps, protecting computer networks and other assets normally associated with information technology (IT). Nevertheless, IT security itself represents a mere subset of information warfare.

Approximately ten disciplines comprising forty individual fields represent the broader information warfare (IW) challenge.[85] Because 4GW represents a universal approach to conflict, the side that employs IW more effectively will be able to conduct efficient battles – whether martial, religious, political, or economic in scope. This bears significantly upon practitioners of 4GCS as both the Islamic jihadists and narco-traffickers, for example, excel at pushing their message across media barriers. With few restrictions on how they wage war, they can practice their trade without constraint. Nation-states that target these groups, at best, apply imperfect strategies.[86] Because of this, such security measures remain more reactionary than proactive.

Corporate security, because it cannot rely upon taxpayer-funded assistance, must adapt on the fly. This rests in direct contradiction of industry practices, which often equate professional certifications and public acceptance as expected standards. Because of the nature of its adversaries, however, 4GCS cannot be defined by such apprehensions. Both terrorists and drug traffickers, as but two prime examples of asymmetrical 4GW threats, benefit from the clandestine nature of their operations. Whereas police – and military – tactics are often public knowledge owing to their reliance upon taxes, 4GW adversaries simply employ competitive adaptation to remain a step ahead of law enforcement intelligence operations.[87]

Information warfare capabilities have accelerated through the benefit of "Netspionage" – the use of "networks and computers and associated capabilities to steal information of a nation-state or other entity

---

[85] Andy Jones, Gerald L. Kovacich, and Perry G. Luzwick, *Global Information Warfare: How Businesses, Governments, and Other Achieve Objectives and Attain Competitive Advantages* (Boca Raton, FL: CRC Press, 2002), 6.
[86] Martin L. Cook, *The Moral Warrior: Ethics and Service in the U.S. Military* (Albany, NY: State University of New York Press, 2004), 35.
[87] Kenney, *Pablo to Osama*, 132.

which can be used to further the aims" of an adversary.[88] Public authorities do not possess this benefit because 4GW entities are usually apparitional and decentralized in nature, leaving domestic and international intelligence agencies with an undetermined threat to add to its collection of potential and probable enemies. IW thus becomes only one slice of the overall 4GW pie. To engage within asymmetrical warfare, practitioners of 4GCS must redefine their concept of conducting battle.

Because 4GW and asymmetrical conflict itself remain controversial subjects within the military studies profession, the reader will now be introduced to a (hopefully) more palatable term, Integrated Tactical Warfare (ITW), as a means of furthering the discussion into 4GCS:

Integrated: Fused, combined, and united into a whole.[89]

Tactical: "Plan of action".[90]

Warfare: "Struggle; conflict".[91]

From this simplistic definition, we can define ITW as a plan of action that involves all aspects of one's life, profession, system of beliefs, training, education, and social ideology into a plan of action for engaging within struggles and other conflicts. This may mean an ability to survive armed battles with insurgents, or it may simply represent a desire for a particular individual to return safely home after a day at work.

Where ITW differs from, say, generic discussions of 4GW, is that it rests upon firm commitments accepted by the practitioner. That is, ITW becomes a mental challenge as well as a physical code of conduct for the security professional that subconsciously prohibits certain actions while allowing others that may, heretofore, have been dismissed by that individual. 4GW, itself, does not bear upon it any particular approach and, therefore, may appear too vague. What ITW does not represent, intentionally, however, is a doctrine for engaging within protective services.

The "doctrine" of ITW simply represents the cyclic and linear influences that every individual proceeds through in life and, often,

---

[88] Jones, Kovacich, and Luzwick, *Global Information Warfare*, 168.
[89] *The Grosset Webster Dictionary, New Revised Edition* eds. William Morris, Charles P. Chadsey, and Harold Wentworth (New York: Grosset & Dunlap, 1966).
[90] Ibid. Definition 2.
[91] Ibid., Definition 2.

overlooked by security professionals.[92]

Figure 5. Influences on Security Providers.

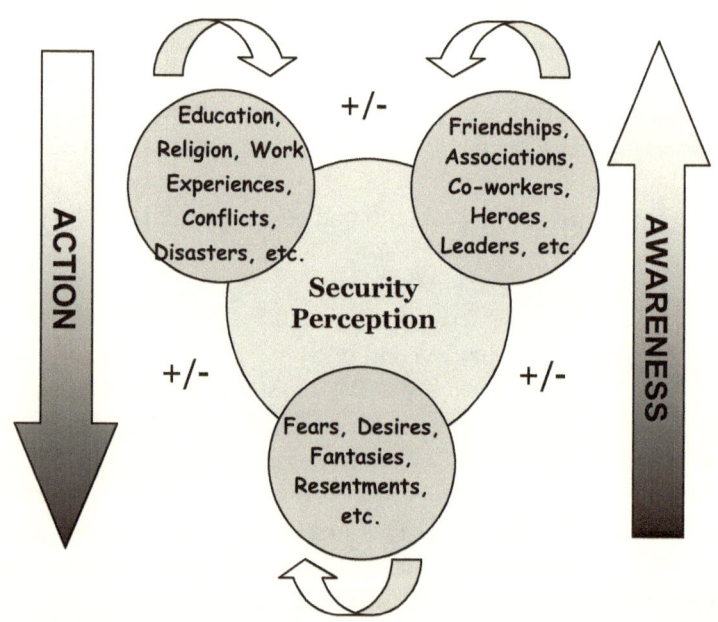

To understand any particular threat, the provider of security must intimately understand how his or her "life" influences his or her decisions. Their awareness may, for instance, be attenuated by a faith-based belief that "God" protects individuals within a church setting, oblivious to the number of Christian churches targeted by non-adherents or secularists. Alternatively, the security professional's awareness could be intensified from being reared within a culture where even religious facilities are repeatedly attacked. A professional's action in response to crises also bears upon his or her background, education, and influences. A former police officer, attuned to centralized bureaucracies may be at a disadvantage in responding to active shooter incidents. Another individual reared within a hostile environment may suffer from fatigue, limiting his or her ability to

---

[92] R.J. Godlewski, "Human Intelligence: Perceiving an Enemy's Thoughts," *American Intelligence Journal* 27 no. 1 (2009): 31.

respond to threats. These twirling – and often conflicting – influences must be analyzed before the 4GCS protective services professional can begin to integrate them into his or her repertoire.

Because no two individuals are similar, no two programs of security can be duplicated. The same company or client may employ each individual, but each bears a different approach to life, business, and leisure. He or she formulates opinions and theories based upon his or her uniqueness, judgments, and *vision*. The latter represents what differentiates groups of security professionals and cannot be learned or developed within a classroom or conference setting. Nor can vision be certified through any professional organization leading to cryptic initials assigned to an individual's last name. This vision – an ability to 'see' beyond that which exists at the present – bonds empirical integration with a tactical plan of action based upon that individual's life.

Terrorists and narco-traffickers employ *mētis* – what the ancient Greeks defined as "experimental, intuitive knowledge."[93] Others, such as sailors, politicians, doctors, and athletes employ their broad range of skills to adjust to life's ever-changing social environments.[94] Awareness of this inherent knowledge permits the security professional to integrate diverse fields (and thoughts) into an effective plan of action the – *tactical* portion of ITW. Most individuals simply consider that which confronts him or her directly and at that particular moment. Security professionals, to the contrary, must consider "presence" in the absolute. That is, they must be continuously aware of his or her surroundings and adjust their thoughts, concerns, and probable actions accordingly.

When a security professional enters a location, they are intuitively aware of exits, potential threats, and a myriad of other factors that may prohibit (or promote) escape from threat. And this activity must be continual, even if a particular location "seems" quite familiar. For instance, just because a particular hallway held six fire extinguishers *yesterday* does not mean that six exist *today*. What if one was stolen? Being used? Out for maintenance? Similarly, an expected exit door may bear an obstacle at this moment that was not there just a few hours before. *Presence* means that the security professional's awareness evolves with time, adding to a base of knowledge already stored within that individual's collective memory.

ITW simply means fighting the war *at hand*. Not the one experienced "last time" or one perceived to happen "in the future". Both conventional militaries and guerrilla bands tend to gravitate towards

---

[93] Kenney, *Pablo to Osama*, 4.
[94] Ibid., 52.

expectations. In Vietnam, U.S. Army General George H. Decker assured President Kennedy that "any good soldier can handle guerrillas."[95] For most of its formative years, "a kind of elite within the elite" Georgetownian crowd that "tended to be well-to-do liberal Democrats" that also viewed Republicans as "cave dwellers" led the U.S. Central Intelligence Agency (CIA).[96] During the height of the Cold War, British MI6 agents employed the wife of the Moscow station chief to meet with a Russian spy.[97]

These examples parallel the aforementioned story about the U.S. Navy forfeiting its war game with the Army because it began its attack on Sunday. Each suffered from ingrained prejudice. During the Second World War, the British tied up German intelligence for more than two weeks by dropping a helium-filled soccer ball, coated with luminescent paint, upon a vaunted Nazi airfield.[98] Beleaguered Nazi leaders could not believe that any pilot would risk his life to drop a ruse upon them, so the glowing, bouncing, and floating ball *just had to be some form of secret weapon* and, therefore, they kept scientists looking for answers beyond the obvious.[99] Sometimes, protective services professionals have to think, "If it looks like a duck and sounds like a duck, then..." *Mētis* permits individuals to adapt to the unknown through intuition, itself a culmination of the five senses.

Speed is of the essence in warfare. One not versed within *mētis* cannot adapt quickly enough to counter a fleeting enemy. In 4GCS, the *conflict/struggle* aspects of ITW remain diverse and diffuse. Islamic extremists, as but one example, often declare that their efforts are, indeed, merely a struggle against the temptations of the world. Nevertheless, many espouse the "three stages of Jihad" – the weakened stage, the preparation, and, finally, Jihad itself.[100] The first stage – long since employed within the United States and Europe – permits Muslims to assimilate peacefully while

---

[95] Harry G. Summers, Jr. *On Strategy: A Critical Analysis of the Vietnam War* (New York: Presidio Press, 1982), 73.

[96] Evan Thomas, *The Very Best Men: The Daring Early Years of the CIA* (New York: Simon and Schuster, 2006), 99.

[97] Victor Cherkashin and Gregory Feifer, *Spy Handler: Memoir of a KGB Officer: The True Story of the Man Who Recruited Robert Hanssen and Aldrich Ames* (New York: Basic Books, 2005), 66.

[98] Arthur T. Hadley, "Maneuver Warfare and the Art of Deception" in ed. Richard D. Hooker, Jr. *Maneuver Warfare: An Anthology* (Novato, CA: Presidio Press, 1993), 364.

[99] Ibid.

[100] Mark A. Gabriel, *Islam and Terrorism: What the Quran Really Teaches About Christianity, Violence, and the Goals of the Islamic Jihad* (Lake Mary, FL: Charisma House, 2002), 85-87.

strongly within the minority.[101] The second stage involves vast preparations in "financial, physical, military, mental" and all other areas required for direct confrontation.[102] Finally, there is actual Jihad, where "every Muslim's duty is to actively fight the enemy, overturning the system of the non-Muslim country and establishing Islamic authority."[103]

Many argue that "jihad" continues to represent nothing more than a personal struggle between an individual and God.[104] While potentially valid, the effective protective services professional cannot take such matters for granted. Two major factors counter the preceding argument. First, there is the concept amongst certain Islamic sects of *al-Taqiyya*, an opportunity to lie amongst "infidels" to hide one's adherence to the Muslim tradition. However one defines the concept, its mere existence opens up a full can of worms. How does one, then, believe a particular Muslim when he or she states that they would *never* harm the host country because *they* are not radical? The mere presence of an official sanction to lie invalidates every argument to the contrary.[105] The second factor involves the existence of the Prophet Muhammad as a warrior.

During his life – which ended under the suspicions of poisoning – Muhammad personally led dozens of military campaigns and authorized many assassinations. His methods were, therefore, diametrically opposed to the Western-centric concept of the Gospel tradition associated with authentic Christianity. Security professionals of the 4GCS type must understand this dichotomy whenever the existence of "peaceful" Muslims is discussed. Yes, the vast majority of Muslims are probably peaceful in nature (again, with the mere existence of *al-Taqiyya*, one has to judge on an individual basis), but it is also argued that the "silent majority" bear very little knowledge on the traditions and laws of his or her own faith.[106] A similar comparison can be made with Roman Catholics, for instance. Church teachings on abortion, female priests, and homosexuality have remained unchanged for two thousand years. Nevertheless, many Roman Catholics in the United States appear to believe that such deviances are permissible under the guise of modernization.

Simply because "the majority" feels one way does not suggest that

---

[101] Ibid., 85-86.
[102] Ibid., 86-87.
[103] Ibid., 87.
[104] Reza Aslan, *No god but God: The Origins, Evolution, and Future of Islam* (New York: Random House, 2006), 81.
[105] Gabriel, *Islam and Terrorism.*, 91-95.
[106] Mark A. Gabriel, *Journey into the Mind of an Islamic Terrorist* (Lake Mary, FL: FrontLine, 2006), 181-186.

the *core doctrine* represents as such. Many do not know that Muhammad, for example, declared that *Trinitarian* Christians – that is, Roman Catholics, Russian Orthodox, mainstream Protestant sects, etc. – were worthy of salvation.[107] Such a belief declares that Christians – who, ostensibly, believe that God remains so *powerful* as to be able to visit earth in fully human form if he so wished – remain polytheists simply because Muhammad, a fractured human being, could not accept such power.

Security practitioners must *continuously* seek out the motives of any apparent threat and this includes determining whether groups of Muslims (or Christians for that matter) are peaceable or militaristic despite common proclivity for granting individuals the benefit of the doubt. War, by definition, remains an offensive lifestyle and, therefore, individuals are going to be offended no matter what charitable peoples are going to do. We shall discuss the religious aspects of 4GCS within the next chapter. For the moment, however, we must consider the martial aspects of religiosity. People who believe in the temporal existence of earthly life will often commit the most ungodly atrocities against his or her neighbor.

Taken as a whole, according to both Sun-tzu and Clausewitz, warfare remains a way of life designed to force others into doing our will. The implications of ITW simply imply a desire to merge one's profession in with his or her personal life – something avowed to by both Islamic jihadists and narco-traffickers. Security no longer remains a part-time endeavor staffed by retirees or young individuals doing coursework on the job. Terrorism and other travesties require diligence. For security, this requires the unified plan of action to deal with *all* conflicts. To aid in authenticating this new 'lifestyle' approach, a strong motivation is required.

---

[107] Aslan, *No god but God*, 101-102.

THE FUEL OF LIFE

Contrary to popular expectations, religion represents the essence of every major civilization from Egypt to Greece to Rome and (in the context of America's founding freedoms) the United States. Religion, in its most basic definition, acknowledges the sacredness of certain practices, locations, or individuals. Some estimates place the non-religious population at approximately one-seventh of the global community.[108] What this means, of course, is that every human endeavor remains influenced by some form of religious belief. Even non-religious entities must deal with this reality, particularly as globalization has become the norm and not the exception.

In 4GW, the issue in question becomes not whether one religious belief is superior to another or even whether one believes in religion or not. The issue remains *how* to incorporate religion as a force multiplier. Most – if not all – cult leaders have employed divine inspiration as his or her ticket to fame and notoriety. Nazi Germany, as but one example, expressed faith in *Der Fuehrer* and caused millions of otherwise rational individuals to trust their future to a maniac.[109] David *Koresh*, leader of the notorious Branch Davidian compound incinerated in Waco, Texas in 1993, assumed the name of Muhammad's tribe (*Quraysh*) to claim descendent status from the Muslim prophet.[110] Even Mormonism (The Church of Latter-Day

---

[108] See http://www.adherents.com/Religions_By_Adherents.html. Accessed February 2014.
[109] Konrad Heiden, *Der Fuehrer: Hitler's Rise to Power* (Boston: Houghton Mifflin Company, 1944), 758.
[110] Haha Lung, *Mind Control: The Ancient Art of Psychological Warfare* (New York: Citadel Press, 2006), 193.

Saints) bears strong resemblance to Muhammad's Islam, sharing nearly identical patterns of belief despite the former's claim of Christianity.

The practitioner of 4GCS need not be a theologian, but he or she must accept reality – religion pervades nearly every facet of human civilization. Nor is it necessary for the security professional to have a solid foundation of any particular religious belief. However, one *must* take care to not trip over insinuations. For example, in writing about the notorious *La Familia* trafficking organization in Mexico, George W. Grayson wrote of the group's Christian books: "It is unclear whether these are King James versions of the Bible or ones that have been embellished by the teaching of La Familia's own leaders."[111] Grayson apparently ignored the fact that Mexico remains 82.7% Roman Catholic, which *does not use* the King James Version of the Bible.[112] Would he suggest that the several books included within Catholic Bibles that are not part of the KJV represents "embellishment" by *La Familia's* leaders? Probably not, but 4GCS requires one to teeter on knowledge without adding to troubles.

The simplest approach is, of course, *not* to dwell on specifics. Many a public figure has been caught in a political vise over whether or not to include the words "Islamic" and "terrorist" in the same sentence. Professionals within the security industry, to the contrary, understand that the vast majority of terrorists attacking the United States and its allies *are* Muslims. Are they *good* Muslims or *bad* Muslims? *That* argument could go on for centuries. The concept of 4GCS – as with any of life's problems – simply acknowledges that Islam inspires these terrorists. When an aggressor uses a baseball bat to assault a victim, one does not need to dwell upon whether that particular individual roots for little league or the majors, or plays hardball versus softball. *Something* (i.e., the bat) of the sport inspired them to commit mayhem. Jihadists are, therefore, inspired by *their interpretation* of Islam – *not* Christianity, Buddhism, Taoism, or Scientology.

What security professionals need to accept remains the *intense devotion* individuals bear towards his or her system of beliefs. Even atheists tend to show defensiveness towards anyone challenging their ideas. What this means is that very few individuals do not believe in "something" greater than him or her – the fundamental basis of any religious perspective. Regardless of whether one believes in an omnipotent God, a series of part-animal deities, a strong central government, or simply in the liberties of freedom (as opposed to, say, free will), religion provides

---

[111] Grayson, *La Familia*, 37.

five key ingredients that practitioners of security must include within his or her analysis of potential threats:

The Five Pillars of Religion:

1. **Superhuman Beliefs:** Not everyone can call upon superhuman strengths to carry them through crises as within comic book fairytales. However, believing in a divine omnipresence provides an individual with the ability to call upon an inherent power equal to that person's level of faith. This is what permitted Saint Simeon Stylites to live atop a 60-foot pillar for 30 years and his followers for nearly twice that long. It is also what permits others to rush into a hail of gunfire to save wounded friends;

2. **A Better Afterlife:** Religion provides the believer with expectations for a more beneficial life after death should he or she die honorably in the doctrine of his or her faith. Many security and military experts fail in recognizing this. David Rooney, a prominent lecturer for the British military, wrote, "What a tragedy for the world that not one of the great spiritual leaders – Abraham, Moses, Jesus, Muhammad or the Buddha – was brave enough to say that he did not believe in life after death. Is this the biggest confidence trick in human history?"[113] Together, Abraham, Moses, Jesus, Muhammad, and Buddha have inspired billions of individuals over the course of a great many thousands of years. Yet, apparently, Mr. Rooney remains wiser than they were. The security professional who practices 4GCS, however, cannot make such bold proclamations; many people actually *believe* certain things that even science cannot define and there remain more individuals who seek this "better afterlife" than deny its existence. *They* remain highly motivated and inspired;

3. **Personal Superiority:** Another British military expert wrote, "...I cannot understand why some people believe that their religion is superior to another."[114] Perhaps such statements reflect from an

---

[112] According to *CIA World Fact Book*, https://www.cia.gov/library/publications/the-world-factbook/geos/mx.html . Accessed February 2014.

[113] David Rooney, *Guerrilla: Insurgents, Patriots, and Terrorists from Sun Tzu to Bin Laden* (London: Brassey's, 2004), 242.

[114] Barry Davies, *Soldier of Fortune Guide to How to Become a Mercenary* (New York: Skyhorse Publishing, 2013), 63.

opinion that the "...British, more candid than we Americans, already call our time 'the post-Christian era'" and, therefore, have lost the concept of religion itself.[115] If we can conclude that religion cannot exist *without the belief in an afterlife*, then we can certainly conclude that *not all religions lead to the same afterlife*. For this same reason, we can conclude that not all athletes prefer to participate within the same sport. With an afterlife defined as some version of "eternity", we can reasonably conclude that each system of belief *must offer something superior to the competition*. This superiority offers the devotee a *reason* to, at very minimum, distrust non-believers. In 4GW, such concepts of superiority remain valid in recruiting, propaganda, and inspiration;

4. **Camaraderie:** There has yet to be, insofar as human history records, a religious system that excludes others. Even narcissists require an audience. As a fundamental pillar of religion, leaders require followers, whether one is Jesus Christ or Jim Jones. Shoko Asahara could not have gassed hundreds of Japanese citizens had his Aum Shinrikyo cult not attracted a stable of pupils. Regardless of the ultimate size of a particular religious faith, its foundation rests upon the impact – largely financial, especially within cults – of adherents. In the smallest of groups, this foundation emerges as an "us versus them" mentality that empowers most illegitimate cults;

5. **Public Influence.** Despite modern inventions as "separation of Church and State", historically religions have existed to influence the broader body of human society. In ancient Mexico, for instance, despite the presence of hundreds of major deities and thousands of lesser ones, an emperor such as Montezuma II held no public cult.[116] However, "religion governed all."[117] What this means is that the religious *system* remained far more important than the semi-divine emperor was. Diaspora Jews survived – and influenced – without the existence of a Temple cult.[118] These examples suggest that any separation between religion and its

---

[115] Peter Kreeft, *Everything You Ever Wanted to Know About Heaven...But Never Dreamed of Asking* (San Francisco: Ignatius Press, 1990), 193.
[116] Hugh Thomas, *Conquest: Montezuma, Cortés, and the Fall of Old Mexico* (New York: Simon and Schuster, 1993), 12.
[117] Ibid.
[118] Martin Goodman, *Rome and Jerusalem: The Clash of Ancient Civilizations* (New York: Alfred A. Knopf, 2007), 426.

environment remain minimal. One cannot segregate a population from the beliefs of its individual citizens. Nor can any security professional dismiss the inherent power of even "impractical" religious beliefs.

Understanding these five theorized pillars remains the foundation of 4GCS. To illustrate this, consider the activities of al-Qaeda and similar jihadi movements.

Few can deny that blowing oneself up or living within caves waiting decades to fight Westerners calls upon a supernatural belief. Similarly, we have all heard stories of "77 virgins" awaiting martyrs in Paradise. Nor can security professionals ignore the fact that Islamic extremists *specifically* target "infidels" underscoring an inherent belief in Islam representing a superior belief and that individual Muslims remain more appreciative of God than even other "People of the Book" such as Jews and Christians. This "against everyone who is not a devout Muslim" leads to strong aspects of tribal camaraderie – so much so that the much sought after Caliphate remains free of non-Arabic customs. Finally, Islamists have been instrumental in influencing public opinion whether it represents targeting individuals who "mock" Islam or employing "lawfare" to neutralize inhospitable cultures and traditions through the court system.

The practitioner of 4GCS must weigh these five credentials whenever they analyze potential threats. Nor can they assume that they will recognize "religion" once they encounter it. Faith often comes under differing guises and, more often than not, dissipates into sects at great odds with the traditional view of that particular religion. For example, Mormonism flowed outwards from Christianity, but it retains very *little* in common with traditional Christian doctrine. Similarly, many cults (in the modern vernacular) such as the aforementioned Branch Davidians masquerade as "Christian" or Christian-like when, in fact, they represent the ambitions of omnipresent opportunists (such as the ill-fated Rev. Jim Jones of the Guyana tragedy). Despite the most common analysis of these cults, security professionals cannot escape the conclusion that the members believed they were belonging to a legitimate religious practice – and by most legal standards, they were.

Fortunately, as with 4GW itself, practitioners of 4GCS bear several tactics to engage these five pillars of religious practice. These methods are not used to defuse or belittle one's religious aspirations, but they are useful in deterring individuals from attacking protected charges. That is, 4GCS professionals can employ these mechanisms to, at a minimum, categorize the threat against them.

Five Challenges against "Fraudulent" Religions:

1. *Do one's "Superhuman" beliefs consciously harm others?* When Saint Simeon spent his three decades living atop a tall pillar of rocks, his actions did not adversely affect others. He influenced either followers or those who wanted to bring him food and take away his refuse. No one's life was irreparably harmed by his method of worshipping God. Contrast this with homicide bombers whose *intent* is to inflict harm against those who do not share his or her beliefs. Similarly, David Koresh's and Jim Jones's self-deification led to the deaths of hundreds of followers;

2. *Does one's hope for the afterlife lead towards the destruction of the present?* All human beings doubt. Even Jesus Christ questioned his influence on rare occasions. That said, doubt does not represent failure to believe. Accordingly, almost every human being desires a safe and prosperous earthly existence. At a minimum, they will care for friends and companions as a way of earning ultimate "paradise". Those religious practices that place others into direct harm remain suspect. Such beliefs hint at ulterior motives, such as *earthly* power under the guise of eternal expectations. For example, the Twelvers ruling Iran who believe that the Twelfth Imam can only materialize on earth *after* the destruction of present society cannot be expected to deliver upon the expectations of that society;

3. *Is the faith superior or simply the self-avowed Leader?* Jesus Christ, the Dali Lama, Mahatma Gandhi, and the Buddha professed divergent faiths. Yet, what all shared was an inherent belief providing a valid message through action of soul. Contrarily, Moses, Muhammad, David Koresh, and Jim Jones waged "wars" against non-believers. This latter group distinguishes themselves from the former by playing action before substance. In fact, Muhammad borrowed heavily from Judaic tradition for his new faith, which is why the sprinkling of heretical Christianity that influenced the Muslim prophet continues to trouble society today. In matters of religion, it is how the leader often *dies* that trumps his or her living. Gandhi and Christ died servants of men. Muhammad, Koresh, and Jones died waging their own versions of war;

4. ***Who are the religion's followers?*** The old adage about being only as good as the company one keeps is extremely valid in deciphering security threats. Only mainstream beliefs attract a wide divergence of followers, which is why only a minority actually understand the true doctrine for which he or she subscribes. Less authentic beliefs attract less authentic personages. Moreover, the more suspicious the doctrine the more likely believers are to be either defensive or ignorant of such doctrine. In this regard, actions very much speak louder than words;

5. ***Is the religion more "political" than divine?*** Inasmuch as all religions affect the public sphere, some remain definitely more political than religious. These groups move far beyond simply "rendering to Caesar what is Caesar's". Often, as within the case of Islamic jihadists, they incorporate every aspect of a person's life into their cause for dominance. In this regard, these questionable religious practices segregate individuals. Most mainstream religious faiths could really care less whether one accepts them or not. Others, unfortunately, do not permit an individual to join or not; they *force* adherence through hook or crook. There remain no prospects for challenge. In this regard, the public exists less as a recruiting pool than as a source of conscripts. Individuals forced to accept particular beliefs remain a serious concern for security professionals.

These challenges do not represent a textbook for confronting illicit religious beliefs. Rather, they represent a guide that should exist within any practitioner's mind when confronting questionable faiths. As such, the security professional should be able to adjust his or her security program. How, then, does one confront religiously motivated criminals and terrorists?

First, one cannot simply criticize the particular belief for doing so grants the adversary the moral "high ground". Secondly, one cannot apply reason (unless they were, say, equitable to Thomas Aquinas) with both the public and the enemy. Islamic jihadists remain exceptional at this, which is why mosques and other Islamic centers have seen a rise in construction within the U.S. *since* the 9/11 attacks. It is also how a group of Muslim students could sue the *Catholic* University of America for maintaining crucifixes upon the university's walls. To counter these methods, security practitioners must employ comparable attitudes. That is, as with all aspects of 4GW, security professionals must "out insurgency" the insurgents.

Again, *all* actions taken against belligerents must incorporate the "underdog" approach.

People, regardless of culture, bear a profound hostility towards authority – particularly alien authority. To defeat narcotics trafficking, for example, security personnel simply cannot rely upon arguments of illegitimacy or employ force. Most farmers growing illicit crops do so for one fundamental reason – they like to feed their families. The *only* qualified alternative remains for security forces to pay higher wages for other crops. Until such an environment can be achieved, indigenous people will continue to conduct whatever agricultural operations financially benefit their families, clans, tribes, etc. The same holds true with indigenous religious beliefs.

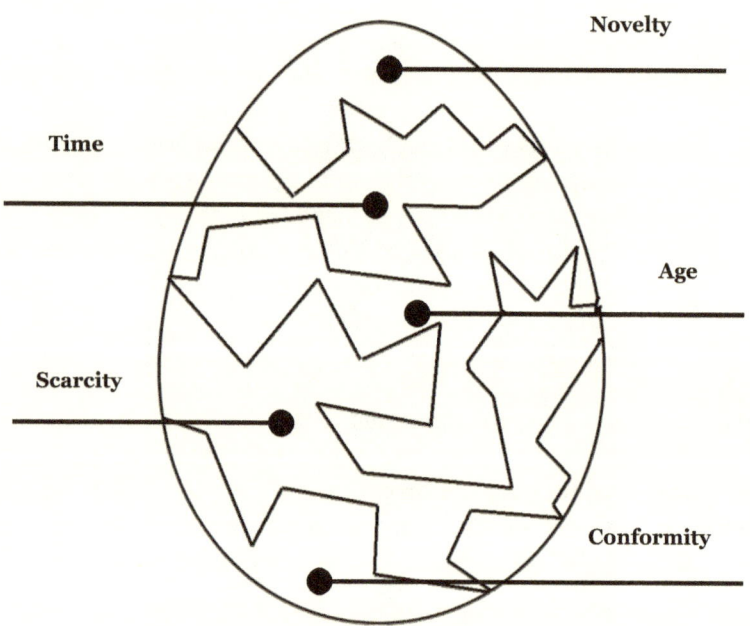

Figure 6. Cracks in Fanaticism.

In order to adequately crack fanaticism in 4GW, five techniques must fit into the perspective security program, building upon the previously discussed challenges and adhering to established principles of blocking "mental bullying".[119] These are not "laws" upon which is based security doctrine, but tactics suitable to individual security professionals challenging fanatical individuals (as in obtaining intelligence from indigenous citizens, incarcerated persons, etc.). As with every aspect of 4GCS, they allow innovation and experimentation in application.

- *Illuminating novelty.* People in the West generally like to try new things, particularly if past, traditional methods have been shown to be troubling or inconvenient. Both advertisers and cults flourish on this, suggesting a 'cure all' technique for calming social ills and personal failures. Some may appear relatively harmless such as when the Gay Rights lobby introduces same-sex marriage in contradiction to 10,000+ years of civilization. Others, such as Muslim Brotherhood instigator, Sayyid Qutb, sought to enforce their agenda upon the world through "the formation of a tightly knit countersociety of believers in the midst of infidel society."[120] The latter subverts through contaminating public preference. The former dilutes through redefining one of civilization's most effective social organizations. The security professional can challenge rising fanaticism through illuminating the break from tradition as an unusual manifestation. For instance, the emergence of radical Islam can be proven as intolerant of other faiths within an open society where success is based upon what works and *not* what merely sounds feasible. New ideas – as borrowed from the scientific method – must be scrutinized as always before acceptance by the broader community;

- *Permitting time.* Fanaticism remains urgent. The alleged 'faithful' bear no time for rational thought for the crisis is *always at hand.* In the case of homicide bombers, for example, his or her death is demanded because 'infidels' are destroying sacredness. Never mind that, in the case of radical jihadists, Christianity and Islam have coexisted for more than 1,400 years. Nor is mention frequently made within traditional religious circles that the "end times" may be thousands of *centuries* off into the future.[121]

---

[119] Lung, *Mind Control*, 51-54.
[120] Abdulkader H. Sinno, *Organizations at War in Afghanistan and Beyond* (Ithaca, NY: Cornell University Press, 2008), 8.
[121] Charles Arminjon, *The End of the Present World and the Mysteries of the Future Life* trans. Susan Conroy and Peter McEnerny (Manchester, NH: Sophia Institute Press, 2008), 14.

Professionals in security and protective services can defuse fanaticism by allowing time to mature. Crisis negotiators handling hostage situations are fully aware that "more time" represents everything in defeating chaotic situations.[122] In 4GW, the target audience is not the enemy; it is the public. Most people do not like to be hurried, which is why used car salespeople and politicians like to make things happen *now*. The rest of the world remains very content with the status quo, which is why 4GCS professionals' goal is for *more time*. By introducing calmness, a sense of posterity (politicians, for one, rarely consider *future* voters), and a remarkable concept of reality, security professionals can show just how "radical" fanatics are;

- *Age remains a gift and not a vice.* The fanatics of the Counterculture 1960's were mostly young people, often college students barely into their adulthood. These individuals were not near the typical maturation age of thirty or older.[123] Because of this, people that better understood their vulnerability bullied them into adherence. Islamic jihadists employ a similar method – believing that a single individual and book (written by Muhammad without criticism) could overrule centuries' worth of doctrine and ecclesiastical conferences by insinuating that the "People of the Book" had *aged* into noncompliance. Even non-Muslims attempt to alter the 2,000 year history of the Roman Catholic Church by suggesting that its core values are "old fashioned". Just because human beings have been breathing for eons does not make oxygen archaic and, therefore, useless. Security providers must commit to the core concept of preserving innocent human lives without segregating individuals into biased preferences. In 4GW, the elderly and young are often targets for appreciation. As such, individual *age* must be of a concern for the practitioner of 4GCS. Accordingly, whenever fanatics indiscriminately target civilians, the youth and the elderly often die and security forces trying to win the 'hearts and minds' of the population must publicize these casualties.

- *The scarcity of life itself.* If time represents a commodity, then

[122] Michael J. McMains and Wayman C. Mullins, *Crisis Negotiations: Managing Critical Incidents and Hostage Situations in Law Enforcement and Corrections, Fourth Edition* (New Providence, NJ: Anderson Publishing, 2010), 152.
[123] Godlewski, "Human Intelligence", 30-31.

certainly human life represents the grandest commodity of all. Because of this value, 4GCS personnel cannot defend *anything* but life. That is, if security personnel even *appear* to be protecting property and businesses to the exclusion of human beings, they will lose the struggle in asymmetrical conflicts. This cannot be overstated because all individuals succumb to this temptation from time to time. Terrorists and narcotics traffickers kill and maim innocent civilians all of the time by nature of the beast. Yet, when *security forces* – whether governmental or private – harm anyone, even the terrorists themselves, they will be perceived as the aggressor in the eyes of the population. Therefore, in 4GCS, all protective services personnel must place proactive force as close to the "firing line" as possible. This reduces the accusations of collateral damage as close to the source as any human can expect ("yes, we shot him...he was shooting at *us* at the time!");

- *Breaking conformity.* Conformity represents little more than "adult peer pressure" and all individuals will yield to majority opinion at least one-third of the time.[124] It is what permits "authority" to turn 65% of the population into willing killers.[125] This reality bears both offensive and defensive implications for the security professional. On the one hand, *belonging* to a religious faith requires one to express allegiance to an established doctrine and a set of rules to follow. One simply cannot be a *true* Roman Catholic, for instance, and support abortion, gay marriage, and premarital sex.[126] On the other hand, individuals are required to delve deeply into their consciousness and determine the best course of action for human decency. During the aftermath of the Battle of Gettysburg (July 1-3, 1863), some 24,000 loaded muskets were recovered with 12,000 found to be loaded more than once, with one example loaded a staggering 23 times without having had been fired.[127] What this suggests is that despite the proximity of authoritative military figures, some individuals simply refuse to kill. Security and protective services professionals need to capitalize upon this and isolate the aggressor from the aggressive philosophy. Here is where research into probabilities of violence is required and every 4GCS practitioner must understand risk

---

[124] Lung, *Mind Control*, 53.
[125] Grossman, *On Killing*, 141.
[126] *Catechism*, #2270-75; #2357; #2353.
[127] Grossman, *On Killing*, 23.

assessment negotiation skills.[128]

Adopting these suggestions into a working security doctrine requires an intuitive understanding of theology, human behavior, psychology, and cultural awareness.

In the 21st century, it remains relatively easy to dismiss religion as a "personal matter" or to believe that a "separation of Church and State" actually exists in law, yet the underlying reality of the human condition remains that the vast majority of the global population still subscribes to some form of religious faith. Religion, arguably, remains a more powerful 'force-multiplier' than even politics – itself a vice created solely to expand upon or supplement individuals' personal beliefs. To accept religion as merely an oddity will force the security professional into a dark corner regarding 4GW operations. Even the Communist Chinese often collaborate with decidedly jihadist elements. The world of 4GCS dwarfs what rests within sight of the human eye.

---

[128] McMains and Mullins, *Crisis Negotiations*, 206-209.

THE VICE OF LIFE

Politics, by any stretch of the imagination, represents an impediment to societal evolution. Political systems come in two basic varieties, open (democratic) and closed (authoritarian or totalitarian).[129] Because 4GW remains apparitional, so too must be the political considerations often formulating its strategies. Political mobilization often erupts along a nation's orthodox social structures since it minimizes the cost and effort of "convincing people to develop new loyalties and patterns of accountability" towards reducing anxieties concerning those who wish to influence an individual's social development.[130] It involves five aspects of power: Love and Respect, Reward, Coercive, Expert, and Position.[131] These categories can be further delimitated into either a tug or push element of political persuasion.

Because politicians must influence divergent personalities, they often seek the broadest element of appeasement. The concept of "political warfare" remains even broader, allowing Sufi Muslim brotherhoods to initiate insurgencies in Algeria and Chechnya/Dagestan and limited governments in Rhodesia and Nicaragua to fend off adversaries besting superpowers.[132] Since political warfare is "generational warfare", it must be

---

[129] Charles W. Kegley, Jr. and Eugene R. Wittkopf, *World Politics: Trend and Transformation, Third Edition* (New York: St. Martin's Press, 1989), 57.

[130] Sinno, *Organizations at War*, 30.

[131] Lung, *Mind Control*, 36-38.

[132] John Ferris, "Generations at war?" in eds. Terry Terriff, Aaron Karp, and Regina Karp, *Global Insurgency and the Future of Armed Conflict: Debating Fourth-Generation Warfare* (New York: Routledge, 2008), 76-77.

ingrained into corporate security on multi-decade level.[133] Clausewitz argues, that "[i]t is, of course, well-known that the only source of war is politics..."[134] Further adding that the unity of human interests rests in "*the concept that war is only a branch of political activity*..."[135] Nevertheless, there remains more to this unity of human conflict than that which is openly seen as politics.

For the uninitiated, "politics" simply represents those activities that govern the state. Others, more traditionally minded, acknowledge that politics represents a "[s]ocial conniving for personal gain."[136] In this regard, we can assume that few political figures seek to serve – at least in the modern era. Politics, despite the size of the host nation, represents a 'big money' discipline that few charitable persons can afford to enter. Moreover, what separates politics from religious faith remains the fact that few, if any, *individuals* can rise to the top without a myriad of supporters representing an inner body of thought and persuasion. Jesus, Muhammad, and Gandhi may have materialized out of a vacuum, but Adolf Hitler, Daniel Ortega, and Hugo Chavez did not rise because of their own initiative.

Because of this fact, politics *can* represent a worse beast for security professionals than even religion. Only slightly, however, and under specific circumstances. Politicians – as opposed to most religious leaders – can impose his or her will upon a significant segment of society. Laws ostensibly prepared for the "good of the people" can be drafted and ratified by very limited individuals. More importantly, few individuals have been bold enough to declare a separation between "Politics and State". These attributes are geared towards war and represent the bond that creates asymmetrical warfare. As an example of this, we need only to analyze the situation referred to as the "Palestinian Crisis".

This eternal problem exhibits several political maneuvers that security professionals need to be aware of. First, there exist no such people as Palestinians. Nor is there an area unquestionably identified as "Palestine". What Palestine refers to is a generalized area east of the Mediterranean and west of the Jordan River that ancient Rome classified as a "territory". *Palestinians* are generally referred to anyone who lived in the region before the modern State of Israel came into existence in 1948 and *specifically* represent Arabs. Therefore, any characterization of individuals as Palestinians tends to focus on the motive of Arab

---

[133] Ibid., 77.
[134] Clausewitz, *On War*, 605.
[135] Ibid.
[136] *Grosset Webster Dictionary*, Definition 2.

nationalization rather than simple ethnicity. This further explains why neighborhood Arabic states collectively target Israel as an intruder despite Jews and Arabs living within the Middle East for millennia.

At its most fundamental level, the conflict between Jews and Arabs arises from Abraham's two sons Isaac and Ishmael and deals with the rights of the first-born in a region where birthrights represent everything.[137] Arabs claim that their 'father' Ishmael deserves the rights of Abraham whereas Isaac, father of the Jewish nation, does not.[138] In the latter 20th century, various Palestinian terrorist organizations have attacked Israel and Jews (and anyone supporting Jews) for simply being *who they were* irrespective of whether or not Jews had been living in the territory occupied by Israel for a great many centuries. More recently, a policy akin to Chechenization – "the profound transformation of a predominantly Muslim society from its traditional, largely pre-Islamic structure to one dominated by Islamist-Jihadist elements that historically have been alien to that society"[139] – has disturbed the Arab-Jewish conflict.

What had been an extremely (leftist) political struggle during the 1970s now involves numerous jihadi groups such as Hezbollah, Hamas, al-Qaeda, etc. whose intent remains more religious than political. Several suspected Chechen operatives have begun to target Israel from the "occupied" territories.[140] While such realities seem to evaporate the political struggle, politics remains the perceived progenitor. In what had been a centuries-long struggle for national independence in Chechnya and Dagestan, for example, now involves Arabs fighting in the Caucuses, Chechens fighting in the Levant, and both fighting in Indonesia.[141] Do Chechens, Arabs, and Indonesians expect the same political system?

As with many aspects of 4GW, it remains extremely difficult to segregate the various sectors. In this regard, it remains best to acquiesce to the basic definition of politics as those beliefs identified with an individual's dealing with other individuals as opposed to one's dealing with the divine. Cults, as an example, are notorious for confusing the two disciplines. The Bhagwan Shree Rajneesh orchestrated biological attack in Oregon was certainly a political event.[142] Aum Shinrikyo's intense bribing of post-Soviet Russian officials in the 1990s also underscored a political objective, namely ceasing surveillance of the cult's activities and acquiring

---

[137] Davis, *Terrorism*, 16.
[138] Ibid.
[139] Yossef Bodansky, *Chechen Jihad: Al Qaeda's Training Ground and the Next Wave of Terror* (New York: Harper, 2007), 2-3.
[140] Ibid., 195-197.
[141] Ibid., 3.

governmental contracts.[143]

Security professionals must examine any potential threat from both political and religious aspirations and continuously examine the other perspectives no matter how practical such considerations may appear. The Taliban, as but another example of an organization purported to represent puritanical religious beliefs, proudly cloaks itself with the prophet Muhammad as a "political masterstroke".[144] As with the political terrorists of the 1970s, today's faith-based groups are not averse to employing political power as required. This appropriation of political intentions can take several forms.

Regarding the narco-trafficking violence in Mexico, one prominent researcher argued, "one relatively *uncontroversial* [emphasis added] solution would be a dramatic expansion of funding for ATF [Bureau of Alcohol, Tobacco, and Firearms] designed to trace weapons used in Mexico to their sources in the United States..."[145] Obviously this suggestion dissipates owing to the *extremely controversial* 'Fast and Furious' fiasco undertaken by the ATF.[146] The politicization of federal anti-gun policies led to at least one federal agent killed and an undisclosed number of firearms handed over to Mexican drug gangs.

Other researchers declare that the situation in Mexico is rapidly descending into a "Waziristan, U.S.A." effect that could lead to millions of displaced "narco refugees" heading northward into the United States. [147] Such a crisis would severely undermine the American political system. The situation south of the U.S. border – extending all the way to South America – has disintegrated due to "...politically motivated and terroristic TCOs and nonstate actors...perpetrating a level of human horror, violence, criminality, corruption, and internal instability..." that threatens the hemisphere.[148] The 1992 Los Angeles Riots and the 1999 "Battle of Seattle" may merely represent modicums of things yet to come.

The rise of human populations and the demise of taxpayer-funded social services due to limited federal, state, and municipal budgets will only

---

[142] Vacca, *Computer Forensics*, 343.

[143] Tucker, *War of Nerves*, 331.

[144] Ahmed Rashid, *Taliban: Militant Islam, Oil and Fundamentalism in Central Asia, Second Edition* (New Haven, CT: Yale University Press, 2010), 42.

[145] Brands, *Narco-Insurgency*, 44.

[146] See http://www.foxnews.com/us/2014/02/11/as-first-defendant-in-brian-terry-murder-is-sentenced-fast-and-furious/. Accessed February 2014.

[147] Paul Rexton Kan, *Mexico's "Narco-Refugees": The Looming Challenge for U.S. National Security* (Carlisle, PA: Strategic Studies Institute, October 2011), 25.

[148] Max G. Manwaring, *State and Nonstate Associated Gangs: Credible "Midwives of New Social Orders"* (Carlisle, PA: Strategic Studies Institute, May 2009), 13.

aggravate the political balance within *any* nation. Such discrepancies lead to other organizations filling the void. Muslim organizations embed a "principle not just to win the souls of converts to the faith, but also their hearts and minds" as a doctrine of religion *and* politics.[149] Hezbollah, a militant arm of the Iranian military by any stretch of the imagination, is itself well versed in the political orientation of the Lebanese population.[150] Hamas, for its role, has determined that the liberation of Palestine from Jews represents a more important goal than developing a universal Islamic society.[151] Both organizations employ social welfare programs to influence their respective communities.

In narco-laden Latin America, the widespread influence of *Los Zetas* appears destined to "incrementally 'capture' the [Mexican] state" through its own political and social programs.[152] Despite the notorious brutality of the special operations-spawned group, "...one can see that these seemingly random and senseless criminal acts have specific political-psychological objectives."[153] These objectives simply represent *Los Zetas'* desire to freely operate within the Western Hemisphere. What confronts the security professional, however, is that *non-state* entities are not the only culprits practicing political asymmetrical warfare. Venezuela has practiced a "type of conflict [that] is primarily psychological-political and aimed at human terrain rather than geographical territory."[154]

Human terrain mapping represents a key aspect of 4GW. One military researcher writes, "In the battle for the hearts and minds, success hinges on our ability to operate comfortably in the psychological battlespace within the gray matter and decision-making apparatus of our adversary. Here we engage and influence our enemy with images and ideas on the human terrain."[155] Certainly, analyzing the ideas contained within human "gray matter" constitute a significant task for security professionals. In the 4GW world, one is "free to indulge in color, symbolism, folklore,

---

[149] Beverley Milton-Edwards, *Contemporary Politics in the Middle East* (Malden, MA: 2006), 136.

[150] Stephen Biddle and Jeffrey A. Friedman, *The 2006 Lebanon Campaign and the Future of Warfare: Implications for Army and Defense Policy* (

[151] Sherifa Zuhur, *HAMAS and Israel: Conflicting Strategies of Group-Based Politics* (Carlisle, PA: Strategic Studies Institute, December 2008), 47.

[152] Max G. Manwaring, *A "New" Dynamic in the Western Hemisphere Security Environment: The Mexican Zetas and Other Private Armies* (Carlisle, PA: Strategic Studies Institute, September 2009), 23.

[153] Ibid., 25.

[154] Max G. Manwaring, *Venezuela as an Exporter of 4th Generation Warfare Instability* (Carlisle, PA: Strategic Studies Institute, December 2012), 9.

[155] Curtis D. Boyd, *Psychological Operations: Learning is Not a Defense Science Project* (Hurlburt Field, FL: Joint Special Operations University, March 2007), 13.

histrionics, and invective!"[156] It is, therefore, only natural for politicians and their staffs to challenge the senses of the average person.

While most Westerners view both religion and politics as subjects for private, personal conversations, the rest of the planet views them as an integral part of life. In the Middle East, for instance, "the arena of informal politics, involving non-state actors, [is where] the most significant Islamification of politics is likely to continue to take hold."[157] These Middle Eastern non-state actors could disrupt the rest of the world through blocking crude oil shipments. Individuals would not even need to create physical chaos to send petroleum markets into a tailspin. Fictive broadcasting in an era of instant communications and social networking would play havoc with the global economy long before national leaders convince a shattered public that the latest crisis never really happened.[158]

Paranoid cultures primed for expectations rather than analyses remain extremely difficult to steer towards the truth. Consider the likely outcome of an Israeli airstrike against Hezbollah strongholds. Who would the Muslim world believe if Hezbollah began to post videos of dead children and wailing mothers on the Internet? The targeted building may have housed the 'Top Ten' of terrorists but it would not matter because the average Arab living in the West Bank, Gaza strip, or even New York City would *assume* that yet another criminal Israeli attack killed dozens of innocent children in front of their mother's eyes (no one ever questions why the *children* died while leaving the grieving mothers untouched to weep in front of the cameras). Cellular telephone cameras will record the "event" and share it with the world long before traditional journalists get a chance to set the record straight.

With the headlong drive towards "digital soldiers", it does not take a strong leap of the imagination to see how bootlegged videos could be turned against these very same soldiers.[159] Security professionals need not only be concerned about fake broadcasts turning public sentiment against global leaders; companies can lose billions from such falsified reports. Already instances of fake press releases caused one company's stock to plummet $45 per share in less than one hour and another's to sink 60% resulting in a market plunge of more than $2 billion.[160] Just imagine the implications of criminality or atrocity. Modern warfare remains a misnomer. Warfare, as always, represents a primal 'winner-take-all' human

---

[156] Balor, *Mercenary*, 217.
[157] Milton-Edwards, *Contemporary Politics*, 266.
[158] Vacca, *Computer Forensics*, 250.
[159] Jones, Kovacich, and Luzwick, *Global Information Warfare*, 534.
[160] Ibid., 13.

endeavor that rarely ceases despite relative periods of "peace" manufactured by politicians.

Typically, individuals never equate politics with war, despite common perceptions of politicians often engaging within "battle" for party supremacy. In this regard, citizens rarely call upon their governments to engage within open warfare unless they have been attacked. Two primary examples of this include Israel after the 1972 attacks at the Munich Olympics and America following 9/11. Where such changes in public opinion affect security professionals deals with the expected change in legislation and national attitude. When a significant event occurs, politicians are bound by his or her function to consider what possible rules and regulations may satisfy their constituents and thus act accordingly. Generally, these new legislations bear little effect upon actual aggressors.

Narcotics trafficking organizations develop *mētis* through extensive, if somewhat informal, brainstorming sessions designed to maximize competitive adaptation whenever counternarcotics agencies strike a blow against them.[161] These changes in operation often come when governments enact legislation to curtail the *previous* methods. Practitioners of security must continuously bear this in mind, for what emerges as a "triumph of legislation" today may simply mean that governments and militaries will be at a loss tomorrow. And any *loss* in 4GCS means that companies, properties, and people will be irreparably harmed as a result.

Furthermore, even within Clausewitz's day, it was relatively normal for nations to sign pacts with one another without actually caring about each partner's success in defense.[162] Groups such as al-Qaeda, however, pounce upon opportunities to challenge the consciousness of civilian populations, to get the public firmly behind the Islamist group under the premise of the latter representing a saving force for helpless and oppressed peoples.[163] Nevertheless, as Poole declares, "...every nation's politics are to some extent America's business."[164] What this means is that American (and, by extension, Western) security professionals have to consider that whatever involves the world will involve his or her security operations whether they understand the implications or not.

Practical security must strip the politics away from any given scenario. To reiterate, "[a] politician promises the voter good government and low taxes when he intends to use government for his own enrichment

---

[161] Kenney, *Pablo to Osama*, 49-75.
[162] Clausewitz, *On War*, 603.
[163] Cigar, *Al-Qa'ida's Doctrine*, 105.
[164] Poole, *Tequila*, 142.

and expects to raise taxes to make that possible."[165] This represents reality whether the politician in question hails from the relatively free United States of America or considerably more tyrannical "democracies" such as the Russian Federation or Venezuela. Because taxes and deceit represent the norm in politics, regulations and interference fail neatly into line. The practitioner of 4GCS, thus, fights the dual battle between his or her quarry and those who attempt to "do good" for the broader public.

As few can do *anything* without adequate capital, the next consideration of 4GW bears, perhaps, more power than either religion or politics. An asset that many declare evil but few desire less of. Capital success, whether free market or otherwise, represents the thread of civilization from the tribal era on through the Monarchial and will not cease with the present fascination with State Capitalism. Commercial warfare, arguably, is the oldest form of conflict known to man outside of basic sibling rivalry.

---

[165] Mack, *Ring of Spies*, 36.

CAPITAL PUNISHMENT

As these words are being written, the nation of Ukraine is literally up in flames as demonstrators in Kiev protest their president's flirtation with Old Russia and the pseudo-Tsarist regime in the Kremlin. Fueling this conflict of preferences between the East and the West rests Moscow's stifling control of natural gas and flaunting of larger purse strings. Nevertheless, Vladimir Putin's tyrannical Russia is not the only country that employs economic warfare as a tool of persuasion. Chinese leaders have declared that they "should use diplomatic, economic, financial, cyber, media/information, and network warfare to neutralize the West's advantages in the military/technical domain."[166] In other words, even massive totalitarian states employ 4GW tactics, especially capital as a means of punishment.

The implications for security professionals remain apparent. Economics represents the virtual lifeblood of business, without which even the most massive institution ceases to exist. Economic vitality pervades all organizations, businesses, lives, and dreams. Turn off – or even reduce – this sector of existence and all other aspects of human life swirl down the cesspool of despair. For this reason, global institutions such as the International Monetary Fund (IMF) and World Bank routinely lend billions to disadvantaged nations.[167] It is also for this reason that Vladimir

---

[166] Thomas X. Hammes, "Response" in *Global Insurgency and the Future of Armed Conflict: Debating Fourth-Generation Warfare* eds. Terry Terriff, Aaron Karp, and Regina Karp (New York: Routledge, 2008), 110.
[167] Milton-Edwards, *Contemporary Politics*, 76.

Putin's resurgent Russia and dynasty-seeking China can coerce poorer neighbors into doing either Moscow's or Beijing's bidding. Money may not be the proverbial root of all evil, but it certainly beckons absolute power.

Consider this scenario within the United States. Approach a motorist and ask them to drive you to the other side of the country and claim that God, or the president, requested the service to be rendered. How many citizens would take you up on the offer? Now, try the same experiment with a suitcase full of $100 bills, and declare that you will provide the driver with $100,000 for the effort. Chances are the motorist would not even care if the money was legitimate or otherwise – a mountain of cash trumps either deity or national leader. In security parlance, he who controls the cash controls the population. Period.

Aside from those fanatical individuals prepared to die for the "Cause", nearly every other entity flourishes upon expectation of profit. Urban populations in Germany during the Second World War readily adapted to 'round-the-clock' bombing by the allies, but it was economic devastation following the First World War that conspired to launch Adolf Hitler into office with a legitimate 84% of the vote. Pablo Escobar's notorious *plata o plomo* – silver or lead – campaign trademarked his dealings with even authority figures.[168] Again, few are willing to sacrifice their lives when the alternative of considerable wealth is available. Even years after his death, Escobar's contributions to his community helped turn his grave into a popular tourist attraction.[169]

Security officials will never be able to match the financial contributions of terrorists and traffickers, if for no other reason than it remains nearly impossible to gauge *who* is to be the target of these illicit charitable works. Nevertheless, proper intelligence provides the *where* security professionals should address for economic assistance. The local community of any facility or operation remains critical in providing early warning against pending attack. These represent the retailers, taxicab operators, newspaper venders, hotel staff, and, of course, beat police officers that intuitively know what is *happening* within the city limits. In the case of law enforcement personnel, "economic conditions affect the workload of criminal justice agencies."[170] This, in turn, leads to "States...searching for ways to reduce spending in order to balance their budgets."[171]

---

[168] Mark Bowden, *Killing Pablo: The Hunt for the World's Greatest Outlaw* (New York: Penguin Books, 2001), 24.
[169] Ibid., plate 23.
[170] Stojkovic, Kalinich, and Klofas, *Criminal Justice*, 61.
[171] Ibid.

Many security companies have been viewed as Godsends that provide services and/or equipment (such as patrol cars that approximate the appearance of legitimate police vehicles) to cash-strapped municipalities without charge. And not only security companies. One Big Box electronics retailer significantly reduced crime targeting a store when its manager offered steep discounts to local police officers.[172] This patronage held an ancillary affect when those same police officers began to overlook minor (and some not so minor) violations committed by store employees.[173] The lesson here is that security professionals can extend his or her intelligence and defensive perimeters as they aid limited-budget agencies in the universal fight against crime and terrorism.

As previously mentioned, the Chinese fully employ economics within their concept of "unrestricted warfare".[174] Hezbollah, for its role, has even been known to recruit high-ranking Israeli officers through payments of both money and narcotics.[175] In chaotic nations such as Colombia, some private security forces take part in money laundering, paramilitary operations conducted on behalf of narcotics groups, and even trafficking itself.[176] Detectives and bodyguards sometimes turn into assassins for transnational criminal elements.[177] These examples merely underscore the need for 4GCS professionals to adapt to economic influence before their adversaries reach strategic advantage. That is, those astute enough to grab the opportunity readily transfer economic concerns for individuals into force multipliers.

Economics – if traditionally viewed as the "Study of the application of wealth and resources to mankind's needs"[178] – permits military and paramilitary organizations to achieve *relative superiority* against an adversary.[179] This concept allows terrorists and transnational criminal elements to plan effective attacks that catch security operations off guard.[180] In broader measures, economic warfare represents the third stage

---

[172] Memorandum for the record, a nephew of author, R.J. Godlewski.
[173] Ibid.
[174] Timothy McCulloh and Richard Johnson, *Hybrid Warfare* (Hurlburt Field, FL: Joint Special Operations University, August 2013), 57.
[175] Turbiville, Jr. *Guerrilla Counterintelligence*, 59.
[176] Graham H. Turbiville, Jr. *Private Security Infrastructure Abroad: Criminal-Terrorist Agendas and the Operational Environment* (Hurlburt Field, FL: Joint Special Operations University, November 2007), 20.
[177] Ibid., 21.
[178] *Grosset Webster Dictionary*, Definition 1.
[179] William H. McRaven, *SPEC OPS: Case Studies in Special Operations Warfare: Theory and Practice* (New York: Presidio Press, 1995), 7.
[180] Stephen Sloan and Robert J. Bunker, *Red Teams and Counterterrorism Training* (Norman, OK: University of Oklahoma Press, 2011), 104-105.

in information warfare, where "intensity of disagreements" spirals into tit-for-tat sanctions, market disruptions, and financial chaos under a convenient cloak of plausible deniability.[181]

If environmentalists declaring the presence of elusive "endangered" species have delayed vast construction projects, just imagine the economic impact of a terrorist front group or criminal-aligned politician spreading rumors about a particular business. To defend against such allegations, security personnel must develop both national and local 'marketing' campaigns to keep the public on the side of the company or organization under protection. While much of this rests with the responsibility of the company itself (security, though, keeps executive management appraised of their responsibilities), several key actions must be implemented.

- The company must contribute to *effective* social welfare programs. Donations to soup kitchens, women's shelters, schools, arts, local sports, etc. keep the brand image of the business in the best possible light;

- The company must keep national media organizations informed of *every* action that affects the broader population (think of the Tylenol® tampering case) *before* crises distort public attention;

- When crises do appear, the company *must* accept responsibility – even if they were not fully implicated – and take proactive measures to "ensure that such things never happen again";

- Corporate management must effectively punish malefactors within its management system while ensuring that such management is not portrayed as "overpaid" bureaucrats;

- Security personnel must always appear as supportive of "the people" even if its primary function remains to serve the Company.

Simple measures often go a long way, and *any* action for which the public views as elitist, exclusionary, or greedy will irreparably harm even the most charitable organization.

The world has passed the point where the punishment for avarice involves execution by pouring molten silver into the culprit's eyes and ears,

---

[181] Jones, Kovacich, and Luzwick, *Global Information Warfare*, 188-189.

but many otherwise decent citizens will still quietly dream of the tactic nevertheless.[182] Islamic terrorists understand this, which is why they employ economic disadvantage as both a plus and a minus in their popular exaltations. During the 1990s, Saudi Arabia developed a surplus of young men reared within a domestic Islamic educational system who could not find work as promised within the public sector.[183] The economic element added to a growing dissatisfaction with Westernization and the appeal of ultraconservative Islamism fueled hatred of governing authorities.[184] From here, al-Qaeda was able to secure recruits who shared Osama bin Laden's extremist Wahhabi ideology.[185]

This anti-Western agenda goes deeper than merely al-Qaeda itself. In 2002, a declaration to a U.S. defense panel read "that Saudi Arabia was an enemy of the United States...that the Saudis were active 'at every level of the terror chain.'"[186] The Saudi government has spent billions of dollars to spread Islamic ideology to "every corner of the earth".[187] Individual Saudi citizens contributed "at least $500 million to al-Qaeda", most of the funding coming from the Kingdom's two largest banks and business families.[188] All this to support an organization whose 9/11 attacks "cost the U.S. economy at least $135 billion."[189] Add to this, that Hezbollah (ostensibly an organization created to oust Israel from Lebanon in 1982) and other Islamic groups operate training camps throughout Latin America to indoctrinate children (as would be homicide bombers) in anti-American sentiments and skill in the use of firearms and other weapons, and the implications for security professionals remains apparent.[190]

The economy – global or otherwise – represents the greatest field of battle for any participant, for the truest nature of war is to make another party unable to succeed. Threatening the Western concept of economic "success", is that much of the non-Western world deals in *hawala*, a personal system of value transfer that permits individuals to literally send

---

[182] Timothy May, *The Mongol Art of War* (Yardley, PA: Westholme Publishing, 2007), 16.
[183] Eleanor Abdella Doumato, "Chapter 2. The Society and its Environment" in ed. Helen Chapin Metz, *Saudi Arabia: a Country Study, Fifth Edition* (Washington: Department of the Army, 1993), 90.
[184] Ibid.
[185] Gerges, *Journey of the Jihadist*, 130-131.
[186] Quoted in Rachel Ehrenfeld, *Funding Evil: How Terrorism is Financed – and How to Stop It* (Chicago: Bonus Books, 2003), 175,
[187] Ibid., 25.
[188] Ibid., 35.
[189] Ibid., 19.
[190] Ibid., 146.

millions of dollars across the planet with very little to register paper trails.[191] This alternative remittance system permits groups such as al-Qaeda to fund their activities outside the vulnerable channels of interstate banking, currency exchanges, and governmental oversights.[192] Hawala thus represents, perhaps, the most secure "economy" on the planet.

Budget conscious security professionals will never be able to target Hawala channels for the only way to disrupt the flow of money is through the elimination or tarnishing of the individuals trusted with the handling of accounts. For multibillion-dollar corporate conglomerates, any attempt to duplicate these transactions remains impossible, if for no other reason than Western expectations of commerce challenge any notion of keeping transactions "off the books". Nevertheless, 4GCS requires practitioners to understand the concept of illicit – or clandestine – economies.

An apparitional adversary will *always* succeed in attacking fixed assets. Hostile groups can accumulate capital and other resources long before they even appear to security personnel as a legitimate threat. The only effective counter to these represents compartmentalizing corporate assets – a burdensome proposition that likely requires board and/or shareholder approval. Still, terrorists and transnational criminals can only target what they find and should a corporation diversify its operations into subsidiaries and divisions not previously known to represent the company, a firewall of sorts can be established between the business and emerging threats.

Consider this situation from a military perspective. During the eighteenth century, armies marched in line formation and wore ostentatious uniforms designed for posturing and expressing an image of bold strength. It remained easy for adversaries to determine approximate strength, leadership, and equipment even from a distance. The battlefield very much represented a chessboard with opposing players defined by specific colors, shapes, and movement. Guerrilla warfare, to the contrary, represents a game of poker with largely undisclosed stakes. Opponents know that the other side possesses an approximate number of cards, but *what* these cards are and *how* they will be played is not immediately understood. Much depends upon the observed skill and habits of the holder.

In a similar manner, corporations can no longer avoid to place all their public eggs into one neat, recognizable basket. New products may have to be developed as "competitors" to the company's previous efforts.

---

[191] John A. Cassara, *Hide & Seek: Intelligence, Law Enforcement,* and the *Stalled War on Terrorist Finance* (Washington: Potomac Books, 2006), 96.

New divisions may have to be launched as completely independent companies rather than obvious expansions of an ongoing concern. It may even prove necessary to "sell" the business to an "outsider" – one prominently engaged within other fields distant to the one under economic attack by disgruntled or criminal elements. Globalization and the Internet are making it rather difficult to conduct business as usual.

Commercial enterprises affect a local economy more than, perhaps, any other social structure. Governments survive through parasitic taxation – conveniently large enough to fund the coffers of bureaucracy but lenient enough to avoid killing the host. Religions survive through offering a bright future with comparatively little sacrifice today and even the broadest faith cannot survive without tithing. Educational institutions survive through charter arrangements with local municipalities or the siphoning off revenues from national and state incomes. Yet, governments, religions, and schools do not necessarily need to remain either effective or efficient to survive. Private businesses, however, quickly collapse once their products or services become too expensive or archaic for the targeted consumer.

The security professional versed in 4GCS cannot isolate economical considerations from his or her battle against terrorists and transnational criminal groups. Chinese triads extort money from stores and enforce these crimes through gang-related threats.[193] Various "Chinatowns" throughout the United States possess a vast "illegitimate underside to business and social life."[194] In writing about the troubles experienced in Northern Ireland, journalist Kevin Toolis wrote, "Economically, there is no merit in any of the republican arguments for the reunification of the island. Northern Ireland is a poor country beset with decaying, unprofitable industries and sustained by massive subsidies from the British taxpayer."[195] Such an environment could only foster grievances and criminality for decades to come.

Russia's own economy palls in comparison to its Soviet heyday.[196] Apparently, such crises at home do not stop Moscow from trying to insert dominance over its neighbors. In this regard, much can be expected from within the security environment of many nations. Economics represents

---

[192] Ibid., 176-181.
[193] Ko-lin Chin, *Chinatown Gangs: Extortion, Enterprise, & Ethnicity* (New York: Oxford University Press, 1996), 73.
[194] Ibid., 13.
[195] Kevin Toolis, *Rebel Hearts: Journeys Within the IRA's Soul* (New York: St. Martin's Griffin, 1995), 25.
[196] Harley Balzer, "Authoritarianism and Modernization in Russia: Is Russia Ka-Putin?" in ed. Stephen J. Blank, *Politics and Economics in Putin's Russia* (Carlisle, PA: Strategic Studies Institute, December 2003), 125.

the fuel of life and a weapon of war. Those with struggling economics – whether individual or national – will seek to disrupt those with more powerful economic opportunities. Socialists prevail in this attack, seeking to control *everything* under the premise of leveling the playing field. It remains this environment *and* weapon that confronts security professionals.

Protective services personnel do far more than just protect individuals and businesses. They protect processes, reputations, ideas, and *economies* as well. Whatever is threatened is what requires protection. An experienced guard at a neighborhood bank, for instance, may seek to prevent trespassers or malcontents, but he or she may not fully understand cyber penetrations or psychological warfare. Similarly, a roving mall security person may anticipate terrorism or active shooters, but he or she may not understand the effect of national protesters demonstrating against the corporate headquarters of a client retailer.

Traditionally, security involves little more than perimeter isolation. That is, a group of security guards is instructed to keep troublemakers out and customers from harming one another while they are 'in' the zone of protection. Very few of a nation's private security force are prepared to confront coordinated paramilitary attackers. If individuals serving within the security profession remain ill prepared to deal with visible aggressors, they are even less likely to deal with "soft", economic assaults. As with religion, politics, and warfare itself, the broad range of threats seeking to destroy any one economy are far too diverse and widespread to categorize into first- or even second-generational marching lines. Criminals and terrorist groups will employ asymmetrical advantage to gain relative superiority during their attacks. Nothing could be easy than for al-Qaeda, Hezbollah, narco-traffickers, or any allied group or individual to disrupt a city, state, or even nation's economic hopes.

TYING IT ALL TOGETHER

Just after the September 1972 massacre at the Munich Olympics, Israeli Prime Minister Golda Meir declared, "We have no choice, but to strike at terrorist organizations wherever we can reach them. That is our obligation to ourselves and to peace. We shall fulfill that obligation undauntedly."[197] Such represents the universal challenge for 4GCS professionals – to strike at terrorist and criminal organizations *wherever they can be reached.* Unfortunately, this goes against the expectations of what "security" entails. More often than not, private security forces are viewed as either occupations that off duty police officers engage within to supplement his or her income or, at the other extreme, "rent-a-cops" that cannot find gainful employment within the *true* profession.

For whatever reason, probably bureaucratic, the misconception that police departments and security companies retain the same function is profound. Yet, police officers and federal agents are *not* qualified security personnel.[198] Nor is their function overtly protective in nature. Well trained within his or her precise field, law enforcement personnel are not well suited for the dynamics of 4GCS and, therefore, should not even be considered when addressing asymmetrical warfare. In discussing a similar problem – that of selecting personnel to represent "bad guys" during training exercises – Sloan and Bunker remind us "active-duty law enforcement and military personnel do not normally make the best red

---

[197] As quoted in Aaron J. Klein, *Striking Back: The 1972 Munich Olympics Massacre and Israel's Deadly Response* (New York: Random House, 2005), 101.
[198] Russell L. Colling and Tony W. York, *Hospital and Healthcare Security, 5th Edition* (Oxford: Elsevier, 2010), p. 159-164.

team members."[199] This is because cognitive dissonance prevents these individuals from "mimicking the behaviors of a terrorist group or lone operative..." due to law enforcement personnel's hereditary "...beliefs, personal biases, and love of country."[200]

Combating terrorism and transnational criminality borders upon breaking indigenous laws (solely because Western laws are as restrictive as to nearly criminalize any individual despite his or her intentions). For this reason, law enforcement personnel generally do not accept duties beyond protecting *and* serving communities. Police agencies are, unfortunately, geared towards response more than action; a trait built into their bureaucratic foundations. The reality of 4GW excludes their participation beyond traditional police functions. Many agencies, for example, throughout the U.S. have been forced to remove religious signage – notably crucifixes – from patrol cars and administrative buildings under the premise that it "offends" certain other parties. In 4GW, to offend is to survive.

Because human history is overwhelming *religious* in nature – from ancient Greeks and Aztecs to today's Christians and Muslims – abandoning religious faith simply denies security personnel the use of a prominent weapon of 4GCS. Religion inspires and influences. It empowers and it challenges. It also keeps the individual *held accountable* to his or her Creator. Religion acknowledges the basis of Good versus Evil; Right versus Wrong; and underscores the concept of Free Will within a world destined to express libertarian freedoms. Yet, religious faith remains *just one* aspect of 4GW.

Human survival also represents a fundamental *martial* challenge. David Livingstone Smith outlines several atrocities within the past ~100 years committed by "The Most Dangerous Animal", including:[201]

- 8,000,000 people of the Congo Free State killed in 1877-1908 by the Belgians;

- 1,500,000 Armenian Christians killed in 1915-1916 by Muslim Turks;

- 5,000,000+ Ukrainians killed during 1931-1932 by Soviet-instigated famine;

---

[199] Sloan and Bunker, *Red Teams*, 73.
[200] Ibid.
[201] David Livingstone Smith, *The Most Dangerous Animal: Human Nature and the Origins of War* (New Year: St. Martin's Griffin, 2007), 217-218.

- 4,000,000+ Soviets killed by Stalin's Great Terror of 1937-1938;

- 300,000+ Chinese killed during Japan's 1937 "rape of Nanking;

- 11,000,000 Jews, Poles, and other "undesirables" killed through Nazi Germany's "Final Solution";

- 1,000,000 Indonesians killed by the government 1965-1966;

- 1,700,000 Cambodians killed during the 1970s by the Khmer Rouge;

- 2,500,000 mostly Hindus killed by the Islamic Pakistani army during 1971 in East Bengal;

- 2,000,000 black Sudanese killed in the ongoing situation in Darfur;

- 1,000,000 Rwandans killed in ethnic fighting between Hutus and Tutsis.

And this represents very much a truncated listed for effect. What if more space were available within this book?

For 4GCS to work, its practitioners must bear teeth within any security program. The millions listed above died because *nobody lifted a finger to protect them.* When police officers and federal agents return home at the conclusion of their typical day, they largely ignore the plight of the world as they tend to their families, hobbies, and other domestic responsibilities. Asymmetrical threats will not turn themselves "off" while you are home with the spouse and children. With the patience of a St. Simeon Stylites, they will wait diligently for decades waiting for that brief moment when *your* guard is down and then they will attack with a vengeance most people never even knew existed within the human psyche.

The reason that most international bodies, particularly the UN, cannot defend the innocent rests largely with the twin attributes of politics and economics. Either it may be unprofitable politically or economically to defend innocent human lives – particularly for those state institutions that try to squash religious duty. Security professionals, however, are paid to *protect*, not follow laws and regulations. True, most personnel will function legally to the best of his or her ability, but when the "other side" begins firing live rounds into crowds, civility dissipates rather quickly. Poole argues that most citizens do not want a bunch of police officers to muster outside a school during an active shooter situation; they want one or two brave souls to enter the facility and neutralize the culprit.[202] It remains argued here, however, that most people want someone *inside* – at the scene of attack – whenever shooters appear. This scenario cannot be practical for police agencies, for, again the only way that law enforcement personnel can protect the innocent is by providing every man, woman, and child with his or her own officer. This is not even possible within totalitarian states.

The concept of 4GCS implies a holistic, lifestyle approach to defending the defenseless. It cannot be segregated into shifts, schedules, or assignments. Nor can illness, injury, or "bad hair" days prevent the security professional from carrying out his or her duty to preserve innocent human lives. As with any military, especially "all volunteer" ones, security personnel accept "the obligation to put their lives and bodies at grave risk" when necessary.[203] Where this obligation distances itself from law enforcement brethren rests with globalization; companies, generally, operate beyond the confines of local municipalities. A police officer in, say, Newark, New Jersey is responsible for entities located in that particular location but remains under no obligation whatsoever to protect people in Sacramento, California.

Conversely, a security professional in Oklahoma City must concern himself with the company's operations in Miami, Florida. Attacks against municipal authority may be relatively isolated, but not threats against corporate enterprise. For example, a disgruntled worker fired from service to Oakland, California is not likely to take out his or her grievances against the Columbus, Ohio fire department. A prominent manufacturer such as General Motors or retailer such as Wal-Mart represents an entirely different situation owing to *brand awareness*. Herein, a disgruntled former employee may build his or her frustration over decades following discharge and may attack *the company* from wherever they reside at that particular moment. They may seek to attack a GM dealership despite that business's relative isolation from General Motors' corporate operations or attack a Wal-Mart truck just because of the name emblazoned upon the trailer.

Because security professionals do not hold such a narrowly defined jurisdiction as do police officers (or even federal agents), they cannot constrict their attention to a particular community or state. Nor can he or she assume that specific taxpayers will kindly provide everything they need

---

[202] Poole, *Tequila*, 182.

to perform their job. The "W" in 4GW means *war*. The security professional must be ready for any threat, at any time, and arising from any quarter.[204] They are *not* soldiers, however, confined to like-minded groups purporting identical training, and benefitting from support staff, medevac helicopters, and political deference. [205] The 4GCS professional is, in all likelihood, an extraordinary *individual*. Whether or not groups of such individuals can form a cohesive group depends largely upon the company seeking protection and the innovation of its senior security officials.

Because 4GW remains cyclic – it bears more in common with primitive vagabonds than Napoleonic armies did with those fighting during World War II – it cannot be categorized into specific elements of criminality or terrorism. Homicide bombers, IEDs, drug trafficking, money laundering, and even active shooters remain mere *tools* of the overall concept. Even terroristic Hezbollah has begun clothing its combatants within distinct uniforms, suggesting an appreciation of conventional military doctrine.[206] This, however, probably has more to do with the group's desire to hold territory and political status than to orchestrate mayhem under the cloak of civilian populations.[207] Nevertheless, 4GCS mandates a martial approach to defending innocents against those whose "tools" break all bounds of civility.

Hardcore terrorists and narcotics traffickers do not care about territory or political standing. Their goals are ideological and profit oriented, respectively. Aspirations for a global caliphate or new markets for cocaine fuel their inhumanity. If beheading innocent civilians and tossing their heads onto crowded dance floors serves their purpose of "only [killing] those who deserve to die", then so be it.[208] If drug traffickers remains as bold as to warn American police officers across the border to "look the other way" while threatening to shoot any off-duty (or, apparently, plainclothes officers) that interfere with their trade, then so be it.[209] These groups do not care who they harm in the process of spreading their "message".

Someone has to stop these individuals regardless of international

---

[203] Martin L. Cook, *The Moral Warrior: Ethics and Service in the U.S. Military* (Albany, NY: State University of New York Press, 2004), 123-124.
[204] Machine, *Security Warrior*, 7.
[205] Ibid., 8-9.
[206] Biddle and Friedman, *Lebanon Campaign*, 45.
[207] Ibid., 73.
[208] Grayson, *La Familia*, 36.
[209] Mark Spicer, "Mexican Drug Cartels: The Growing Threat of the Sniper Attack", *The Journal of Counterterrorism & Homeland Security International* 16, no. 4 (2011): 49.

diplomacy and courtesy. This is where the traditional classifications of security guard and protective agent diverge with the latter emerging closer to warrior than ever before. While 4GCS relies almost exclusively upon the dedication and devotion of individuals, the field itself must be built system-centric. No longer can security be merely content with "guarding". It must strive for *protecting* at all costs.

Unfortunately, many security contractors – particularly those lending services in Iraq (and Afghanistan) – have soured the industry as a whole.[210] These problems, it should be remembered, arise from *any* comparable "gold rush" period. Where 4GCS overcomes this reality, rests with the fact that its practitioners cannot be motivated by money – which is a fleeting and highly subjective commodity. After all, those motivated by money will certainly adjust loyalties whenever someone *else* ups the ante. This explains why political terrorists and drug trafficking organizations remain exceptionally paranoid in their respective duties. Security professionals *must* adhere to the principals that govern their "grave duty" to protect innocent human life.

To succeed in this, 4GCS requires the practitioner to coalesce around four distinct arenas:

Table 3. How aspects of 4GW fit into 4GCS.

Intelligence

Intelligence provides the security professional with an absolute awareness of his or her strengths and weaknesses and provides an opportunity to gauge threats and formulate plans of action.

Tactical Training

A warrior remains useless unless he or she becomes proficient in the tactics of conflict rather than merely the weapons of war. The "Olympic" sport of 4GCS rests with threat resolution and every practitioner should strive for gold through repetitive training and self-discipline.

Community Service

Service to humanity should be the first priority of the security warrior, for his or her "grave duty" rests with the propagation of freedom and the opportunity for life.

Business

The client of 4GCS remains businesses, corporations, and other dynamic institutions engaged within commercial enterprise. To serve is to know, and no security professional is of use unless he or she fully understands commerce and free market enterprises.

---

[210] Steve Fainaru, *Big Boy Rules: America's Mercenaries Fighting in Iraq* (Philadelphia: Da Capo Press, 2008), 62-63.

These segments of life are, naturally, simple extensions of fourth-generation warfare and interconnect in a *sphere* of awareness that encapsulates the professional's life.

To serve a community requires intelligence gained about that particular community and this, in turn, fosters capital appreciation. To protect both businesses and communities requires tactical aspects not fully understood by proverbial "guards" casually checking ID badges and guiding children into classrooms. Business, however, promotes advanced technical training and demands greater situational awareness, which, again, leads to a requirement for more intelligence. A cycle of life that continues on *ad infinitum.*

In the beginning of this book, intelligence was discussed following a chapter on ethics. In this regard, these represent the foundation of successful life: knowing everything that is possible to know about one's chosen path and possessing the decency to travel that particular path both honorably and sincerely. This concept of honor "is central to warriorship" and represents "a concept common to all warrior groups, regardless of the cultures in which they formed."[211] Forrest Morgan's words suggest a profound separation between "security guards" and 4GCS warriors. The first implies a part-time job whereas the latter mandates total commitment.

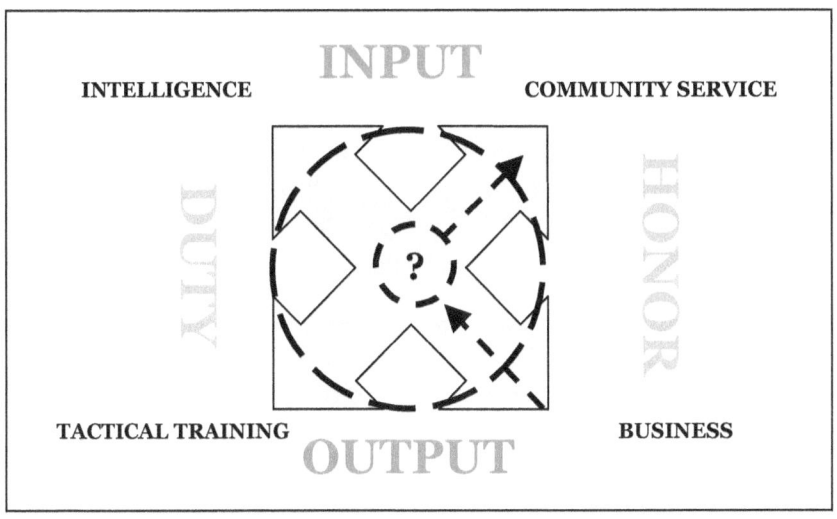

Figure 7. Resolving 4GCS issues.

---

[211] Morgan, *Martial Way*, 140.

As with all human endeavors, 4GW and 4GCS cannot isolate themselves from the broader chaos of human activity. This is why HUMINT – *human* intelligence – rests as the core discipline of practical security operations. Without *actionable* intelligence, practitioners simply retreat to caricaturization as "rent-a-cops". Proper intelligence extends the threshold of warning far beyond the facility or asset under protection. In an era where customers can track retail purposes across the country and know precisely when that package will arrive at his or her front door, security professionals often remain in the dark regarding potential threats. While it remains impractical to expect anyone to sit in front of a computer and watch terrorists or criminals tracked along well-defined schedules, it should not be beyond the security professional's capability to *anticipate* the arrival of certain threats based upon specific situations.

Actionable intelligence begins with the 'Big Picture', a daily consideration of what is happening within the world. Unfortunately, our senses are not objective; people tend to observe what they believe they see.[212] Individuals also suffer from cognitive biases – mental errors free from emotional and intellectual predispositions.[213] Compounding the problem rests the sheer volume of information available to an individual based upon his or her specialty.[214] These occurrences cloud our judgment regarding potential threats and their likelihood within our environment. This is, perhaps, best reflected within the ageless adage about everything looking like a nail to a man possessing a hammer.

Mention terrorism, for instance, and everyone today – particularly U.S. politicians – are likely to recall al-Qaeda. Yet, all but the most scrutinizing professional fails to consider that the nexus of al-Qaeda rests with the Jalaluddin Haqqani Network ("Haqqani Network") in Afghanistan and Pakistan.[215] Haqqani's original "jihad" began in 1973, matured during the Soviet invasion of Afghanistan in 1979, and culminated with al-Qaeda's ongoing war against the West.[216] The volume of information, and opinions, available regarding terrorism in the 21st century obscure the archaic nature of the tactic. Individuals seek well-defined persons matching cognitive biased expectations rather than envisioning the evolution of aggressors.

Similarly, many security professionals today cannot – or, possibly, will not – draw a connection between atheistic China and savagely

---

[212] Heuer, Jr., *Intelligence Analysis*, 7.
[213] Ibid., 111.
[214] Ibid., 51-52.
[215] Don Rassler and Vahid Brown, *The Haqqani Nexus and the Evolution of al-Qa'ida* (West Point, NY: Combating Terrorism Center, July 14, 2011), 18.
[216] Ibid., 18-19.

monotheistic Islamists.[217] The more astute simply remember the line about common enemies making strange bedfellows. China, largely through Chinese Americans, has been involved in drug smuggling and other criminal vices since the late 19th century.[218] The presence of al-Qaeda, Hezbollah, drug traffickers, and Chinese military advisors throughout the same Latin American countries is not coincidental. It has been suggested that Chinese involvement in Afghanistan could be a ploy to redirect American interests away from Beijing's aggressive attitude in the Western Pacific.[219] This situation between non-religious regimes and overtly Islamic ones is not new; the Soviets courted many Muslim nations in the 1980s and Iran's Ayatollah Khomeini once considered an alliance with the USSR to target the United States specifically.[220]

Intelligence operations within 4GCS must consider all potentialities, no matter how seemingly inconsequential or impractical. Just because, say, Islamic jihadists promote a purified version of their religion does not mean they will avoid drug production and smuggling if it furthers their cause against the West. Criminal organizations require vast sums to affect their trade and who is to question *where* they receive this money? The 4GCS practitioner thus considers the world as his or her stage. Despite the theatrics of 4GW, the script is definitely all business.

Corporate security *is* corporate business. It is neither governmental nor charitable in nature. Because it represents capital enterprise, 4GCS must be both efficient and timely. Pearl Harbor and 9/11 attacks severely bruise nations, but they do *not* destroy them. Yet, a relatively minor attack against a corporate entity can severely cripple its operations (consider the recent cyber attack against Target retail stores). Time, therefore, is of the essence in corporate security. So, too, is an appreciation of business management. Frequently, the average citizen pays very little attention to the demands and realities of free market capitalism. He or she remains likely to view corporations as greedy or, perhaps, antagonistic without understanding how private investment, risk acceptance, and ingenuity fuel the economy.

Intelligence, charitable awareness, and business acumen simply outline the tactical requirements for 4GCS. What happens when a threat materializes? More importantly, what do security personnel do when the

---

[217] H. John Poole, *Dragon Days: Time for "Unconventional" Tactics* (Emerald Isle, NC: Posterity Press, 2007), 3-23.

[218] Michael Kenney, "The Architecture of Drug Trafficking: Network Forms of Organisation in the Colombian Cocaine Trade" *Global Crime* 8, no. 3 (2007): 238-239.

[219] Sinno, *Organizations at War*, 269.

threat in question places innocent human beings into direct harm? Sadly, most security texts merely cover the *infrastructure* of security guard operations. At best, they defer to a carefully crafted emergency management system to mitigate the consequences of incidents.[221] In the case of terrorism, all discussion of proactive measures involves *what the terrorists plan and execute.*[222] Other books simply discuss countermeasures in the form of, say, protecting structures against terrorist attacks.[223] In these more specialized texts, "force" is often relegated to a very brief paragraph regarding the "exercise of arrest powers".[224] Deadly force – emboldened for effect – "is reserved for life-threatening situations, *never to defend property* [emphasis added]."[225]

While essentially true – property can be replaced, human lives cannot – these brief flirtations with the worst of humanity lead to false assumptions that security represents an antiseptic industry. It is not. Executive protection (EP) professionals, to the contrary, train to expect the unexpected.[226] One tactic that they employ is to redirect attacks against their principal.[227] This action remains far more proactive than simply 'guarding', but it may not go far enough. Many security professionals – as well as most citizens – believe that aggressors are merely trying to scare their victims.[228] This represents a grave fallacy, one that may land innocent individuals in the morgue. In protective services, as in broader security, "[e]nding up in court beats ending up in the morgue."[229]

Given the nature of modern terroristic and criminal threats, 4GCS professionals should assume on spending a great deal of time in court following major incidents. The mere thought of employing advanced tactics and weapons, aggressive response, and, most of all, direct offense action leaves one exposed to a range of civil and criminal liabilities. Nevertheless, the basis of 4GCS rests upon the notion that human life *must be protected wherever it finds itself in jeopardy*. And by *whatever means may be necessary*. Again, security professionals' actions must always align with the intention to *save lives* and not kill others, even if killing the aggressor

---

[220] Ibid.., 107n15.
[221] Fay, *Security Management*, 259.
[222] Ibid., 435-446.
[223] Purpura, *Loss Prevention*, 184-184.
[224] Ibid., 88.
[225] Ibid.
[226] Benny Mares, *Executive Protection: A Professional's Guide to Bodyguarding* (Boulder: Paladin Press, 1994), 37.
[227] Holder and Hawley, *Executive Protection*, 15-16.
[228] Ibid., 73.
[229] Ibid.

remains the most likely and advantageous outcome.[230]

Proper employment of 4GCS rests with the development of an appropriate operational *system* – "the rules, procedures, and protocols that govern your behavior" – reflective of the environment through which your individuals will be operating.[231] The key here is *individuals*, while 4GCS requires exceptional individuals, no *single individual* can command the moral and operational obligations offered by asymmetrical warfare. This may appear confusing, but it rests upon basic military logic – each individual must strive for personal perfection in order that unit cohesiveness matures and validates itself. Any 4GCS operation cannot tolerate the existence of what Couch warns against as "pirates".[232]

Poor characters arise within any organization, given enough time to foster, but the inherent limitations on the security profession dictate that there are not enough resources within any one operation to overcome the dishonesty and unprofessionalism of these malcontents. Furthermore, unlike virtually all other security-related disciplines, 4GCS represents very much a *clandestine* endeavor. This, itself, may appear shocking in today's open and permissive society, but the diversity of 4GW mandates a secretive approach to protective services. Whereas community service and business activities are undertaken to prepare a company in the best light, proactive measures designed to safeguard individuals and "punish" aggressors cannot be as publicized.

Consider this scenario for a moment. A homicide bomber approaches a school bus full of kindergarteners and, just before they are able to detonate their device, an alert security professional takes him or her down with a well-placed shot above the third thoracic vertebra. One dead terrorist and dozens of safe children (not to mention a bus that lives to see another day). The situation could have involved a terrorist or drug trafficker preparing to detonate an improvised nuclear device (IND) and the survival of an entire city would not have mattered. *Someone* would try to turn the tables on the security professional and make the bomber out to be the hero. A few parents can also be counted on to sue the security company – and not the bomber's family, the school board, or even the municipality – despite the fact that the security professional saved their very child. This ironic twist almost certainly happens in any such event.

Nor does it seem to matter to anyone that according to some experts such as Yossef Bodansky, bin Laden's al-Qaeda had acquired "more

---

[230] *Catechism*, #2263.
[231] Machine, *Security Warrior*, 19.
[232] Couch, *Tactical Ethic*, 106-110.

than twenty" suitcase nuclear bombs from the Chechens.[233] According to Bodansky's quotation of senior Pakistani intelligence officials, "at least two nuclear weapons may have reached U.S. shores" around the same time as the 9/11 attacks.[234] Whereas some readers may quickly dismiss such allegations, practitioners of 4GCS cannot. His or her duty remains *to protect innocent human lives*, not kowtow to public authority or legal grievances.

How, then, do security professionals merge the martial, religious, political, and economic aspects of 4GW into a clandestine operation? Much the same way that terrorists and transnational criminals do: accept responsibility for what appears good and deny implications for those things that disgust the public. Survival represents a battle for publicity as much as it does for existence. Any entity engaged within 4GW must appear both powerful and durable. Because asymmetrical conflicts outline various discrepancies in all parties' character, "truth" becomes subjective. For example, if one side's personnel strengths are superior, then the opposing side must inflate truth to reflect that its forces, though much smaller, actually reign stronger or more efficient. Conversely, if an opponent bears a greater cyber warfare capacity, then the weaker aggressor must present indifference to information technology operations (while simultaneously building an appropriate cyber capability).

In clandestine warfare – indeed, within any psychological operation – lying remains the preferred tactic when the truth may lead to injury or death.[235] In 4GCS, however, the preferred tactic remains to *conceal* the truth; not to supplant it. A security team conducting tactical training operations, for instance, does not need to publicize the story that they are merely conducting "red team" operations (which would seem odd if they were dressed like an American SWAT or military unit). The team simply needs to conduct its operations away from the public eye. Where deception would come into play rests with a fair degree of posturing.

Let us suppose that the threat under consideration represents the presence of narcotics gangs moving into rural territory. Here, a brief newspaper or television story about the "elite security team demonstrating their 'raid and ambush' skills" might just go a long ways towards swaying the narco group into occupying some other unfortunate territory. Or, perhaps, the demonstration of a "new electrified corridor" being installed within a local bank might persuade would-be robbers to target another

---

[233] Bodansky, *Chechen Jihad*, 102-105.
[234] Ibid., 104.
[235] Consider, for example, Genesis 20: *New American Bible*. Also, *traditional* Islamic Interpretations of *al-Taqiyya*.

enterprise. In each case, the "truth" was stretched for strategic advantage. Neither of these cases is possible, however, if the *true capabilities* of the security team were known.

What *is* beneficial for publicity; fortunately, represent the "good things" a company or business does for the local community. After all, 4GCS warrants the "hearts and minds" of the local population. A 4GCS operation in rural Colombia probably does not match the raw firepower of *Fuerzas Armadas Revolucionarias de Colombia* (FARC) guerrillas. That said, new agricultural businesses sprouting in the area may offer local farmers an opportunity to move away from more illicit crops. All that it takes is one or two individuals to accept the legal alternative to provide security specialists with another node in the intelligence pipeline. The key here is that 4GCS personnel must "sprout up" as if they were *always* there. Few people like interlopers, xenophobic society or not.

For 4GCS to be effective, its practitioners must sign off on the following considerations:

✓ **What martial aspects must be enacted?** What can the security operation get away with? What must not be implemented under the laws and regulations of the environment within which it operates? Do we possess enough personnel and material to challenge the threat *if* presence turns into aggression? Does the cost of court outweigh the prospects of death?

✓ **How can we maximize the benefits of religious faith?** How do our operations compare with the expectations of a culture steeped in religious beliefs? How can we underscore our desire to *save lives* rather than destroy them? More importantly, do *our* religious beliefs aid us in enduring the "long war" that represents 4GW? Can we sleep at night knowing what we have done during the day?

✓ **How do our operations affect the political fabric of society?** Will national leaders view us as friends or enemy? Will our operations inadvertently lead to more legislation against private security companies? How will the *media* characterize our mission? Will our activities irreparably damage the corporation or institution that we are committed to serve? Most importantly, are we prepared to do what is *right* – even if it remains fully unpopular?

✓ ***What are the economic implications of our mission?*** Do our activities damage people's livelihoods? How much revenue will our company or business lose if we continue with this? Will our operation cost more than the benefits that it provides? Is this activity or operation even *necessary*? If enacted, can this *reduce* costs in the long run (through training, repetition, dissolution)?

In the field of security and protective services, 4GCS represents the most *demanding* occupation to consider. Balancing upon the brink of open warfare requires sound mind, agile body, and exceptional devotion to duty. It is not for the lighthearted, but neither is human life itself. Modern security services remain "a grave duty for someone responsible for another's life, the common good of the family or of the state."[236] This "grave duty" leaves no margin for error.

For this reason, security can no longer be left to "rent-a-cops". Nor can protection be left to either military or police forces that remain bound to represent a nation or municipalities' conscience. At some point – and you may well decide whether it has come or not – the threshold of warfare has been crossed by private security professionals charged with the protection and preservation of innocent human lives. If not, then *who* can accept the "grave duty" to protect life? In the immortal words of Edmond Burke, "The only thing necessary for the triumph of evil is for good men to do nothing."[237] The sword of 4GCS must be sharp enough to slice off this evil so that the underlying society can begin to heal.

---

[236] *Catechism*, #2265.
[237] http://www.brainyquote.com/quotes/authors/e/edmund_burke.html. Accessed February 2014.

URBAN SCENARIO

As of 2010, estimates place 75% of the global population as residing within urban areas.[238] That a comparable percentage of commercial enterprises reside within urban environments cannot be dismissed. The importance of the world's cities rests upon their representing "centers of finance, politics, transportation, communication, industry, society, and culture."[239] Such a densely populated environment suits 4GW and, accordingly, represents a critical field of battle for practitioners of 4GCS. It is here that religious, political, and economical opportunities often erupt in martial expectations.

Cities arguably represent the worst possible terrain upon which security, law enforcement, or military forces could respond to crises. Unlike jungles or, especially, desert and woodland topography, urban centers depict the only *three-dimensional* setting likely to face corporate security personnel. Aircraft can only be controlled from within or from the ground and mountains and trees offer relatively minor changes in short-distance elevation. Only dense urban centers offer a vertical climb of a sheer 1,000 feet exhibiting upwards of 100 stories (and potential dangers) or more.

Further confronting security professionals are corporate facilities, consisting of both the aforementioned skyscrapers and other diverse industrial and retail establishments. Each particular facility offers not only scores of potential threats, but resides within a densely-packed arena

---

[238] Department of the Army, *FM 3-06.11 Combined Arms Operations in Urban Terrain* (Washington: Headquarters, Department of the Army, February 28, 2002), 1-1.
[239] Ibid., 1-7.

populated by hundreds of thousands of individuals, 65% of which bear the capacity of killing your protected charge.[240] Making matters more difficult, most cities – even within the United States – prohibit many of the tools and tactics required by 4GCS. What, then, do corporate security professionals do when, as in the case of a prominent Michigan mortgage company, their employer decides to relocate thousands of workers into the relatively confined area of downtown? Either they quit in protest or they simply accept the illogical move and do his or her best to protect under the new arrangement.

In an ideal situation, corporate security personnel would have prevented the company from relocating to a major city despite the brief accolades offered by the press and city planners. Placing thousands of employees into a constricted area – with executive offices overlooking a main thoroughfare no less – represents the *worst* move a suburban company could make. All that it would take is one passing vehicular bomb detonated at an inopportune time to destroy that company's operations and kill hundreds of people or more. At best, a lone gunman firing a high-powered rifle (or comparatively low-powered "assault weapon"[241]) could stake out key executives and target them easily during dawn and twilight when interior lights shine through mirrored glass. As the case of the D.C. snipers proved, urban terrorists do not even need to target a fixed structure to "fry the brain" of businesspeople.[242]

Urban centers require astute 4GCS awareness, compounded by the population densities of cities and towns throughout the world. These locations are not similar to rural areas where, as in the days of America's founding, buildings served as outposts fortifiable against marauding raiders. On the contrary, commercial enterprises located within city limits pose very little warning between the presence of hostile individuals and their opportunity to strike. The structure of urban society itself merely magnifies these challenges.

People living within the world's towns and cities factor in several considerations encountered throughout his or her day. The larger the urban environment, the more homogeneities decrease and society devolves based upon government and politics, demographics, health, historical, leadership and personality, ethnical and cultural, religious, and economical

---

[240] Grossman, *On Killing*, 141.

[241] The term "assault weapon" represents a misused term employed by the media and certain politicians mainly for shock value. *Any* weapon employed during an attack, whether knife, baseball bat, or even flintlock musket could be so termed. It is used within this book for the reader's convenience.

considerations.[243] Any one of these elements bears the capability of destroying security for a commercial enterprise. At best, they foster grievances as society descends into cliques that compete against one another for dwindling resources. As these populations expand, the availability of taxpayer-funded services will decrease proportionately leading to fewer jobs and escalating into a 'runaway' effect of poverty and resentment.

Security professionals cannot acquiesce to the appearance of calm within his or her particular city. As with the case of Seattle during 1999, chaos can erupt unexpectedly from any progenitor. As with Los Angeles in 1992, such an eruption feeds off others joining the fracas with very little knowledge of *why* that particular riot began. During one relatively calm period, a large retailer in Arkansas closed a downtown store, offering three days of "bargain sales" for the consumer. By the third day, the 'sale' turned into a virtual riot with "consumers" carting away anything that the building contained including lighting fixtures, shelving, and shopping carts.[244] What the company had envisioned as a surefire way of depleting stock turned into a rapid free-for-all that undoubtedly caused more damage and injuries than that business anticipated for the whole of the store's existence.

Security and loss prevention personnel for the troubled retailer should have recommended (forcefully) a better strategy for liquidation, one involving a controlled sell off, perhaps duping the customers into believing that stocks were low due to late deliveries and the ongoing "sale" was simply a way of clearing discontinued merchandise. What the retailer managed, however, was to thrust psychological bullying – employing *novelty, scarcity*, and *time* ploys – upon an unsuspecting and ill-prepared population.[245] Without having sufficient time to think about the consequences of his or her actions, the consumer encountered a unique opportunity to save money on purchases (novelty) during a "going out of business sale" (scarcity), and knew that they only had three days (time) to act. The result was a mini-riot that left the building gutted and dozens of shoppers injured.

To adequately plan for urban security, 4GCS professionals would do well to examine the history of Rio de Janeiro. That Brazilian city bears

---

[242] John West, *Fry the Brain: The Art of Urban Sniping and its Role in Modern Guerrilla Warfare* (Countryside, VA: SSI, 2008), 285-300.
[243] Department of the Army, *FM 3-06 Urban Operations* (Washington: Headquarters, Department of the Army, October 26, 2006), 2-13.
[244] Memorandum for the record, R.J. Godlewski. 2001.
[245] Lung, *Mind Control*, 52.

over 1 million slum dwellers, possesses an extraordinarily high murder rate (topping one victim per 700 residents each year), and experiences at least four kidnappings per week.[246] European and North American cities may not escape this fate if municipal budgets are not corralled in favor of market-based capitalism. That Rio de Janeiro will host the next summer Olympics in 2016 should be a concern for all security professionals.

Sarajevo hosted the Olympics in 1984 as part of Yugoslavia. By 1992, Yugoslavia began to crack and descend into madness with Sarajevo under siege by Serbs.[247] The carnage culminated in the city hosting a "Sniper's Alley" with literal tourists allegedly arriving to shoot down innocent human beings for sport.[248] Human depravity has not ceased with the advent of modern conveniences. On the contrary, the primal nature of human brutality assures us that the future will remain as barbaric as ever.

As recently as 2002, violence in India between Muslims and Hindus resulted in mothers impaled in front of their children, other young women raped in the middle of the day, and one pregnant victim having her belly torn open with her fetus raised upwards by the tip of a sword before being tossed into a raging inferno.[249] There remains little mention of where "security" was during such atrocities. Such cannot be the case for practitioners of 4GCS, who more resemble caged dogs eager to get after intruders more than family pets that may become riled *only* if their masters are attacked. Modern security must develop a more anticipatory function than it had in the past.[250]

To develop this anticipatory nature, security professionals must be fully active within the four arenas of 4GW conflict *on a community-wide basis*. The fundamental responsibility of 4GCS rests with the company or principal under protection, but this does not diminish the responsibility of the security professional from realizing this requirement across the full spectrum of networks, associations, opponents, rivaling philosophies, etc. that make up the particular city he or she works within. To understand this obligation, we must turn to that all-encompassing field of intelligence and how it relates to a corporate entity's defensive perimeter. From here, we can examine several potential urban crises and how to mitigate destruction and disruptions from these occurrences. The reader will be permitted sufficient leeway in determining his or her precise response as it relates to

---

[246] U.S. Army, *FM 3-06*, 3-16.
[247] John West, *Fry the Brain*, 238-240.
[248] Ibid., 242-250.
[249] Smith, *Dangerous Animal*, 29.

their particular situation.

Figure 8. Urban landscape. © SeanPavonePhoto - Fotolia.com

Because urban environments represent a massive maze through which any number of threats may materialize and befuddle corporate protective services personnel, security must avoid a linear system that fails to consider both aerial attack and subterranean (e.g., sewers, subways, etc.) fronts. The best approach, therefore, remains to extend a security group's intelligence network far beyond the urban center (that is, where the three-dimensional sphere *shrinks* to a lower plane). From here, security analysts can determine which threats are likely to emerge within office buildings, industrial factories, and dispersed retailed establishments. This will not, unfortunately, eliminate uncertainties involving *existing* threats within a company's sphere of operations, but threats that are more aggressive are likely to materialize from distant locations.

The first step in building the security intelligence network rests with identifying the particular "norms" for the location. This simply entails sending individuals out into the city to observe the ebb and flow of pedestrians on a daily basis. Most people, lacking prudent security

---

[250] See R.J. Godlewski, *Anticipatory Corporate Security.*
http://rjgodlewski.com/AnticipatoryCorporateSecurityByRJGodlewskiTACTICALEXT
RACTIONSSecurityPaperJULY2012a.pdf.

consciousness, settle into predictable patterns. They leave to work at the same time, use the same route, shop at the same gas stations, and eat lunch at the same restaurants. While observing and analyzing every single motor vehicle remains nearly impossible, detecting oscillations in traffic is not nearly as difficult. Over time, individuals tuned to the "organized chaos" of daily traffic *can* isolate disturbances much as how a discerning art critic can pick out blemishes within an otherwise immaculate painting or a musician can hear a flattened note within a chorus of instruments.

   The individuals best placed to detect these minor alterations of society represent those located in *specific* locations or occupations. Police officers, for instance, gain a feel for their beat and intuitively know when criminals break habits. Convenience store clerks are often privy to those who appear "lost" and require assistance in finding addresses. Certain taxicab operators become aware when drivers begin to seek out other routes than the ones they held for, say, the past several years. Waiters notice when regular customers change mannerisms or cleanliness. This information remains inconsequential in and of itself, but 4GCS professionals need to focus on the "big picture" and that picture may be comprised of millions of smaller bits.

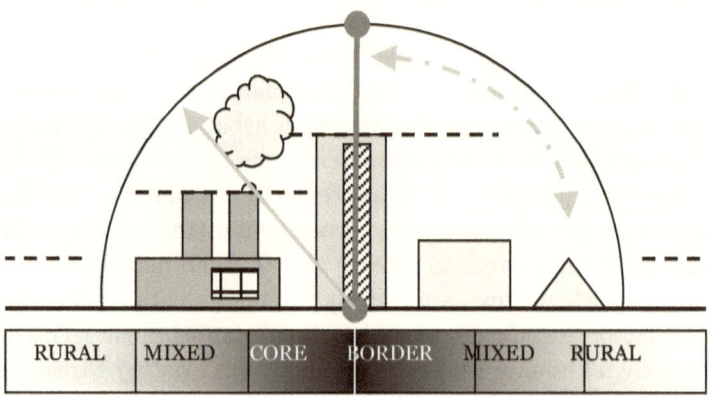

Opportunities to gain height advantage over security forces declines with distance from urban centers, as few tall buildings exist in suburban areas. This permits security professionals to refrain from focusing on 'aerial' attacks in outlying areas. It remains important, however, to take the pulse of activities within these high-rise, human dense locations.

Figure 9. Reduction in dimensional threats further from urban
   center. Characteristics include outlying rural residential
   developments, mixed-use and core peripheral, and central core
   urban models.

Security professionals are likely to neither possess the intelligence gathering capabilities of nation-states nor acquire the supercomputers that massive data draws require to analyze, but this represents an advantage in fourth-generation and asymmetrical warfare conflicts. In fact, Pearl Harbor, Korea, Vietnam, Iran, Lebanon, Grenada, Iraq, and 9/11 all represent American conflicts in which intelligence failed the United States. What security professionals need to develop is best described as a "voodoo intelligence doctrine".[251] This concept exists when the information received comes in tattered bits and pieces that, upon first glance, do not make much sense. They play around in a person's mind while they are driving home from work or while shaving. At the most unusual time, perhaps after letting oneself loose out on the town, the implications of the data figuratively smack him or her straight between the eyes and a virtual "Eureka!" moment announces a broad recognition of enemy intent.

In this regard, "voodoo" intelligence remains little different from traditional intelligence practices. Where divergence comes, however, rests within the recognition that "official" intelligence agencies rely too much on technology and advanced computers while leaving too much to the interpretation of bureaucrats. As an operative of 4GCS , *you* are the one responsible for intelligence successes and failures. Nevertheless, these 'bits and pieces' of information do not come easy. They arise when you wade through the local shopping mall and you begin to understand that the pair of women arguing over a pair of slacks may be debating the cost versus the color. Or when you realize that the individual shuffling his feet in the cosmetics store is waiting for his wife to make a decision. Perhaps, even, as you sit in a booth sipping your second cup of root beer, you notice a man nervously back up in a corner of the mall, his clothing not quite fitting to his body.

Human intelligence comes from all sources and at all opportunities. What it does not come with, however, is an explanation. Rarely do individuals fully announce his or her true intentions. Even police investigators and criminal interrogators realize that most of what they hear is false and misleading. To safeguard their charges, security professionals have to determine the intent of *everyone* they meet and this may involve millions of people in some global megalopolises (urban centers with populations exceeding 10 million residents). Can a single individual or even an entire security operation know the true intent of literally millions of people? Frankly, no. At least not simultaneously and uninterruptedly.

What security professionals within the urban environment can do,

---

[251] Balor, *Mercenary*, 229.

however, is *compartmentalize* this sea of potential threats. City inhabitants can be categorized into four broad classifications, each of these further subdivided into likelihood of aggression, criminality, or perversion. To begin, let us consider *who* inhabits a city at any particular period.

- **Permanent residents.** These individuals live within the city confines and rarely depart. They may be young professionals who deem public transportation more cost advantageous than buying their own vehicle, artists that enjoy the 'loft community' of many neighborhoods, or the homeless whose lack of a proper residence keep them glued to the slums of the inner city. Whomever they represent, they spend more than 75% of their time within the city core (usually for work or vagrancy) and core periphery (primary residences). These individuals generally define the *culture* of any particular city;

- **Transient residents.** These individuals either live within the city on a temporary basis (e.g., college and university students) or reside within secondary homes (such as diplomats and executives) that are more convenient than that individual's primary house. Transient residents, because they do not characterize their urban domicile as permanent, generally do not affect that community. They do, however, *absorb* both the culture and the attitude of the city in which they live. Because they bear an opportunity to *choose* living where they do, they do not often add to either the culture or the attitude of other individual residents;

- **Transient workers.** Not to be confused with migrant workers, transient employees work within the confines of the city core or periphery, but they reside outside in the suburbs and further. He or she may boast about their urban affiliation (e.g., sports teams, music, food, etc.) but do not possess sufficient loyalty to actually reside within the city limits. Because of this strong affinity without due loyalty, they contribute (and largely invent) the *attitude* of the city. The foregoing two groups may consider this pack as "wannabes" at best, and interlopers at worst. At any rate, the association represents a mixed blessing for they provide revenues for the city and, yet, often determine its future through legislation and/or development.

- **Tourists.** Tourists represent everyone who finds him or herself in the city at any particular time without a permanent need to be there. They may be on true vacation or simple layover during extended travel. However they find themselves within the city, they are not likely to announce their presence beyond a qualified 'need-to-know'. Their stay can be as long as a week or more, but they neither exhibit a preference for their location nor absorb any of its culture and/or attitude. They are simply "there" and when they leave, they will not think twice about their visit or announce plans to return. A presence within that particular city just represents a casualty of travel.

With these groups in mind, we can ascertain the potential for each individual to engage within criminal behavior, terrorist attack, or other deviant behaviors.

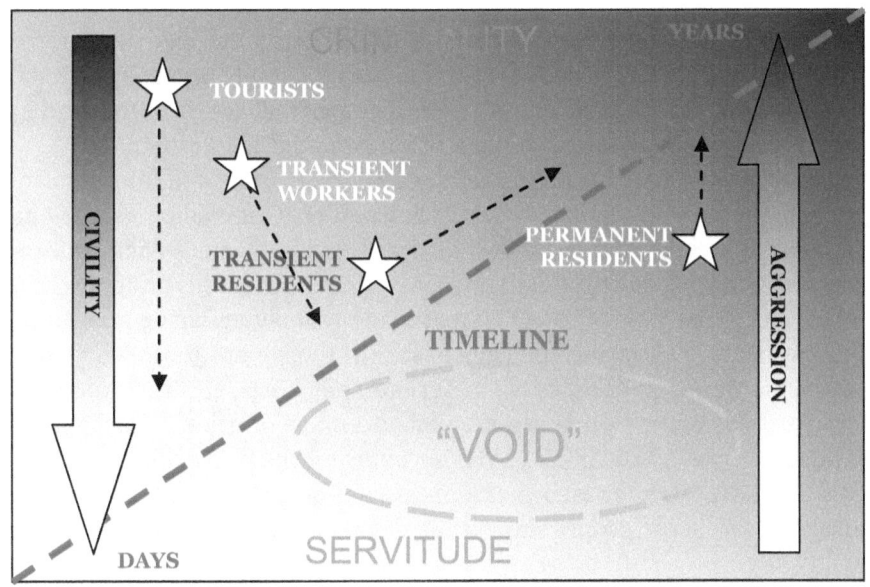

Figure 10. Potentialities for Aggression.

As we can observe within the above illustration, each of the four groups of inhabitants begins within a fixed point and migrates towards his or her acceptance or rejection of that community. For example, permanent residents begin within the societal pressures of the city, but as stable inhabitants, his or her move towards aggression is unlikely to mature very far. As they build towards aggression, they also innovate methods with which to endure this stress. At worst, permanent residents tend to become bitter and intolerant rather than overtly violent. Occupying the opposite end of the spectrum, tourists launch into anxiety by mere presence within a foreign or unfamiliar city. Novelty makes every individual a bit recalcitrant. However, this nervousness quickly dissipates once they acclimate to their surroundings. Several factors aid in this process. First, there is the relatively short duration of their stay. Those on vacation have conducted some research beforehand and, therefore, understand what to expect. Others that may be on layover understand that his or her presence is extremely brief and very often restrict themselves to the confines of an airport or hotel.

Secondly, tourists – as with anyone embarking upon novelty – remain on the defensive for the duration. This defensiveness could turn violent if confronted, but it stays any action as they seek to gain control of their emotions. Finally, tourists simply do not know *who* is friendly or not. Aggressors rarely target *everyone*, which is why the "bully" syndrome does not work against superior numbers. Brief visits to the city often force ordinary citizens to acquiesce to "good behavior" simply because he or she is not prepared for any alternative. Acting properly allows them to blend in and, therefore, not raise any response from potential aggravators.

There are, naturally, exceptions to every rule and the security professional must understand these peculiarities. Criminality, as but one example, flows through the timeline. Psychotic individuals may venture into a neighboring city to commit atrocity within hours of his or her arrival. Others may finally "snap" after a great many years of enduring grievances and hardships. Occupying the calmer side of society are those who value true servitude – ministers, missionaries, nurses, priests, etc. Their inherent compassion – not everyone can succeed as a nurse or priest – keeps them ground to longevity and civility. This accounts for the void, which increases over time. [Note: the presence of a diagonal 'timeline' exists because with advanced age, *most* people show some degree of aggression or decreased civility.[252]]

These considerations grant the practitioner of 4GCS an opportunity to plan effective intelligence networks within his or her city. By intuitively understanding the *structure* of the city – the three-dimensional topography of humanity – the security professional can understand *where* and *how* individuals congregate. Upon this, he or she can superimpose expected behavior models – the potentialities for aggression map – to gauge which segments of society are primed to instigate conflict with other

---

[252] McMains and Mullins, *Crisis Negotiations*, 394-406.

neighborhoods. With practice – and a great deal of patience – these activities become known. The microcosms of disruption become readily apparent to the well-trained eye (and mind).

Certain threats announce themselves so brilliantly that they remain ignored by everyone who should know better. Several stories, for instance, mention of the 9/11 hijackers seeking to learn to fly – but not *land* – commercial aircraft. In December 2007, two men of Middle Eastern descent enrolled within Indianapolis-sponsored Emergency Medical Technician (EMT) courses sought to learn more about *hospital communications* and *response measures* than those subjects that were required for state certification.[253] Similarly, in October 2007, suspicious individuals touring the area in a yellow rental truck were noted by a Maywood, Illinois hospital security staff discussing the location as "ground zero".[254]

These examples illustrate unusual behavior for otherwise seemingly normal human beings. The practitioner of security must flag these occurrences as anything but innocuous. To achieve this, his or her intelligence operation must include the *"Mousseblin"* – taxi drivers, store clerks, newspaper carriers, students walking home from school, *anybody* that can make sense of what is normal or not (insofar as people pay attention to details). These bits of information and rumors build into perimeters of security surrounding particular locations.

- **Crisis Perimeter:** This represents all company owned and/or controlled properties. Here is where the question "How can staff, contractors, and visitors be in danger?" In 4GCS, this is the *martial* perimeter where direct action may be required to apprehend or neutralize trespassers.

- **Defensive Perimeter:** This corridor represents the broader community surrounding a *particular* facility such as an office building or industrial plant. If the company does not entirely own the building (as in the case of many large office structures), then the defensive perimeter shrinks down to those spaces that the company directly controls. The question in this environment remains "What *could* be threatening my facility?" and involves a direct conflict between pedestrians or traffic with corporate operations.

---

[253] Indiana Department of Homeland Security/Indiana Intelligence Fusion Center, *Suspicious Activity Involving Emergency Services and Hospitals*, June 2008.
[254] Ibid.

- ***Intelligence Perimeter:*** This boundary extends from those areas that intermingle with corporate properties (i.e., the cities and states where operations are based) outwards to include the entire planet (and even outer space if you are concerned about either asteroids or surveillance and communications satellites). The primary question for this sphere remains "What threats have I overlooked before?" and represents an evolutionary consideration.

These spheres of awareness build upon a security professional's human terrain models and piece together a "best guess" scenario of potential threats. As with a ball, floating upon the water, one particular scenario or event adjusts the security system protecting the company. What is *not* overlooked, however, is the need for security to bear assets *in* these perimeters. Security professionals must know when and how these threats are encroaching upon company territory and this cannot be achieved at the terminus. Nor can anything be dismissed as commonplace or innocuous.

A small child dashing out in front of your car may simply be an inconvenience or a well-orchestrated ploy to get you to stop at the sight of an ambush. Those environmental protestors complaining about climate change in front of your gate may simply be misguided students seeking a better world or they may be carefully selected instigators set to disrupt your company's new product rollout. Security must always keep its finger on the pulse of both the local community and the broader world influencing those inhabitants. To achieve this, it must place intelligence collection as far out into the world as possible.

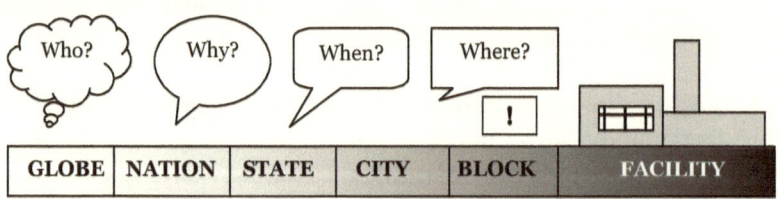

Figure 11. Progression of Concerns towards Corporate Facilities.

With limited budgets and personnel, security departments cannot possess enough individuals and technologies to create an all-encompassing intelligence blockade around any particular facility. They can, however, recruit the services of traveling salespeople that can provide indications of how the company is viewed in foreign locations or neighboring states. Truck drivers, for their role, present a unique ability to provide all-source –

human, communication, image, electronic, etc. – intelligence throughout most of the contiguous United States. They can provide security departments with a range of perceptions about what is happening in other cities and even along the borders because, on average, most over-the-road drivers run upwards of 750 miles per day. Attendance at security conferences also provides professionals with an opportunity to gauge the whom, why, when, and where of potential threats.

Once threats materialize and take action against company facilities is when 4GCS professionals distance themselves from garden-variety security guards, for 4GW mandates a *martial* element within life. This is also where some heavy soul-searching is required of the protective services company. When crises emerge, do they retreat and cover? Blockade and await law enforcement? Or do they draw the proverbial line and defend human lives *at any and all cost*? Frankly, 4GCS requires the latter. Under *no circumstances* should security personnel delay a moment when innocent human lives are at stake. To do so simply announces to the world that "Your Company" remains ripe for the picking.

Urban environments, unfortunately, make such actions nearly impossible for the diversity in political beliefs they entail. Certain East Coast U.S. cities, for example, have all but legislated terrorism and transnational criminality into supremacy. When tragedy strikes, their first rule appears to be to enact further laws upon law-abiding citizens. Such 'knee jerk' reactions explain why 4GW adversaries include politics within their arsenal. Instead of empowering a community or state to fight back, a brief attack remains far more likely to have bureaucrats eliminate the tools necessary to support either law enforcement or security companies. Nevertheless, security professionals must remember the "grave duty" they inherit when accepting the job. Politicians and governmental bodies can be sued when they interfere with basic human survival. Innocent lives cannot be recovered once they are killed.

Because of this fundamental obligation to protect innocent human lives, 4GCS personnel cannot place undue concern on "breaking the law" when lives are at stake. For example, no one would question someone from breaking into a building to retrieve fire extinguishers when a school bus full of children is ablaze. Nor is any jury likely to convict someone who bludgeons a pedophile to death during his or her process of raping a small infant. Juries – if properly selected from a group of one's peers – tend to remain apolitical in the course of their duty. What, therefore, are the *tools* available to 4GCS teams that may not be available for traditional security guards?

One of these tools remains better armament than that likely to be used by terrorists and transnational criminal elements. At least, these include weapons more efficient in defending against these radical criminal elements.

Figure 12. "Urbanized" Ruger SR-556 Rifle in 6.8 SPC. © R.J. Godlewski

One of these weapons – often ignored by state and municipal governments – is rifles that can *defeat terrorists* in the urban environment. Handguns and even shotguns may not provide proactive security personnel with sufficient – and practical – firepower. The urban theater of operation requires neither high-powered rifles nor scopes, nor does it require long-distance battles.[255] In Grozny, Chechnya, Islamic extremists were fighting Russian soldiers by literally shooting through the walls and ceilings of the room they were occupying.[256] Naturally, security professionals – *including 4GCS operatives* – do not condone rabid shooting within confined spaces. Yet, since terrorists and drug traffickers *do* commit atrocities, *someone* has to be prepared to engage and stop them.

In Figure 12 is a representative solution to unwanted terrorist elements. Unlike the prototypical AR-15/M-4 that has been the mainstay of American military and law enforcement agencies since the 1960s, rifles such as the Ruger SR-556 (in 6.8mm SPC) photographed above offer unique characteristics that make them superior to smaller caliber rifles. Fitted (as with the above example) with a 4x32 power, illuminated mil-dot reticle scope, three-point tactical sling, and forward mounted vertical grip and bipod, such a rifle can provide *trained* security professionals with the range necessary to engage urban targets without the massive penetration offered by larger, high-powered rifles. Such a weapon – and a great many others – further serves as an effective counter sniper or hostage rescue weapon without relying upon a dedicated and more costly rifle. Furthermore, rifles such as the Ruger SR-556 represent piston-operated

---

[255] West, *Fry the Brain*, 22.
[256] Ibid.

firearms – meaning that they do not accumulate as much dust and debris within the chamber, keeping these rifles functioning cleaner (and longer) than standard AR-15/M-16 firearms.

Such recommendations – merely suggestions for illustrative purposes – are *not* for every security program within the United States. Close Quarter Combat (CQB) operations are *solely* for those security operations that can afford or gain access to workable situation training ranges.[257] These ranges should include realistic targets (such as those sold via www.letargets.com) and the shooters should employ frangible rounds to avoid harming innocent souls through ricocheting bullets.

Less enthused security companies can still employ tactical handguns and shotguns bearing, if preferred, non-lethal rounds to engage aggressors or even sabot rounds in their shotguns to disable vehicles. However, the emphasis *must be on "rendering the aggressor unable to inflict harm"*.[258] Otherwise, protective services personnel simply provide security for the terrorists and criminals creating mayhem. The move – albeit a highly controversial one – to tactical response units (TRU) represents the apex of internal intelligence operations.

Figure 13. Interconnectedness of 4GCS Urban Operations.

---

[257] Mark V. Lonsdale, *Advanced Weapons Training for Hostage Rescue Teams* (Los Angeles: STTU, 1993), 7-32.

The key to success within any urban crises encountered by 4GCS personnel remains the complete and successful integration of a functional intelligence fusion center, the design and use of an effective tactical training center (sometimes erroneously labeled as "kill houses"), and the application of coordinated TRU groups. These units are not necessarily as complex – or expensive – as taxpayer-funded operations but can still provide security services with a sharpened edge that, at a minimum, will provide terrorists and transnational criminal elements with something to think about before they target a particular company.

POINTS TO CONSIDER

- Terrorists and transnational criminals routinely employ Google Earth and alternate reality sites such as Second Life to plan and rehearse their attacks. This leaves security at a disadvantage because they will not be aware that their facility is being targeted until it may be too late.

- Jihadists will use the law against communities, effectively playing the 'victim card' in order to have local governments do their bidding at the expense of indigenous taxpayers. This is problematic in regions where "religious freedom" forces others to acquiesce under the fear of bigotry and discrimination.

- Municipalities sometimes resemble the parents of squabbling siblings. They do not care about what is right; they just do not want anyone creating chaos and spoiling their day.

- Urban environments provide security personnel with three-dimensional challenges – threats may arise from above as well as from below and 4GCS personnel must understand the city's high-rise structures as well as its subterranean drainage systems, gas mains, etc.

- To survive in 4GW, security personnel must be trained and prepared to employ *martial* force when necessary, despite hesitations against using such "deadly force" in society. Terrorists will not be as accommodating.

---

[258] *Catechism*, #2266

MARITIME SCENARIO

A full seventy-one percent of the planet remains covered with the ocean. This proximity to the sea bears significant implications for security professionals. In the troubling Middle East/Northern Africa (MENA) region, every nation is accessible from the sea.[259] In Latin America, most major urban centers are equally accessible from the sea along with many national capitals serving as ports.[260] In the Far East, only Mongolia remains landlocked.[261] Upon these seas travels the vast majority of the world's trade goods, from basic foodstuffs to automobiles, kitchen appliances, electronics – and millions of tons of illicit narcotics.

As with any industry that produces billions in revenue (take your pick of currency), the trade of the sea attracts every violent, illicit economy that an individual can imagine. The emergence of numerous "free trade" pacts eliminated border obstructions for many of these illicit activities.[262] Few, if any, nation-states can patrol the entirety of their coastlines, leaving passage to those criminal enterprises who can afford to place strategic surveillance along their prized smuggling routes. The practitioner of 4GCS confronts two primary vices when his or her attention turns towards the sea: smuggling and piracy. Unlike any strictly terrestrial obligation, these maritime threats represent the most violent and well-organized criminal enterprises of 4GW to be encountered by security professionals.

For convenience of discussion, these dual threats will be defined

---

[259] U.S. Army, *FM 306.11*, 2-2.
[260] Ibid.
[261] Ibid.
[262] Davis, *Terrorism*, 10.

as:

- **Smuggling**. The clandestine transportation of contraband, primarily consisting of illicit narcotics, arms, and individuals, across national borders with the intention of inflicting harm upon an unsuspecting population and/or deriving maximum profit from the endeavor.

- **Piracy**. "...an act of boarding or attempting to board any ship with the apparent intent to commit theft or any other crime and with the apparent attempt or capability to use force in the furtherance of that act."[263]

For its role, piracy represents at least $12 billion dollars in annual losses for maritime businesses and the nations they serve.[264] The monetary transactions of smuggling are incalculable. So, too, are the human casualties of these twin abominations.

To prevent harm from occurring to his or her charge, the security professional must develop a keen appreciation of 4GW, most notably its martial and economic implications. Political and religious aspirations remain apparitional within the maritime environment; with so much money literally floating around, virtually no actor exhibits any strict religious doctrine and few politicians remain honest in comparison. This money represents "an economic and political institution that motivates people [and] shapes nations."[265] During the Spanish colonization of the Americas, "...smuggling came to rival storms at sea as a cause of..." financial ruins for those exploring the New World.[266] As another example of human vice destroying human society, Western importation of opium into a weakened Chinese economy devastated the lives of countless individuals who turned to the "morally repugnant" narcotic to soothe their concerns about life.[267]

It remains easy to understand that security professionals face a difficult task when confronting either smugglers or pirates for each bears a hereditary career for many individuals. Such occupations are often aided –

---

[263] Michael McNicholas, *Maritime Security: An Introduction* (Burlington, MA: Butterworth-Heinemann, 2008), 161.
[264] Jim Gray, Mark Monday, and Gray Stubblefield, *Maritime Terror: Protecting Yourself, Your Vessel, and Your Crew against Piracy* (Boulder: Paladin Press, 2011), 1.
[265] Timothy R. Walton, *The Spanish Treasure Fleets* (Sarasota, FL: Pineapple Press, Inc., 1994), *ix*.
[266] Ibid., 84.
[267] Ibid., 198.

not corralled – by nations with exposure to the sea. In the context of 4GW, security professionals will not win such conflicts in either the political or the religious realm. With billions at stake, no political body on record bears a sincere intent to defeat either smuggling or piracy. If the security professional attempts to approach matters on religious grounds, they remain likely to suffer defeat by entities better in tune to matters of faith. Accordingly, security professionals can only fight trafficking and pirates on marital and economic grounds for these represent the two fields where *pain* is felt.

To consider the substance of these threats, consideration must be directed towards cocaine trafficking from South America, principally the smuggling operations that developed in Colombia. The rise and fall of Pablo Escobar first developed and then dispersed the modern methods of the cocaine production network.[268] The actual architecture of drug smuggling involves various loose 'wheel' and daisy chain networks.[269] Several of the nodes within smaller networks include individuals functioning as leaders, investors, buyers, recruiters, packers, enforcers, trainers, couriers, and wholesale distributors.[270]

The production and smuggling of cocaine had long drifted away from what most government and media personalities erroneously characterized as "cartels".[271] The disintegration of Escobar's Medellin group, followed soon by the break-up of his Cali competitors in the 1990s, left the narcotics industry fragmented into smaller, more specialized groups that today both compete against and support one another as deemed necessary.[272] Very often, these mysterious business associations are lumped together under convenient terms and structures to further domestic and international political agendas.[273]

What truly exists, however, is a dangerous mix of confined territorial space, illicit commodities fueled with "dirty money", and an impenetrable communications network of digital signals.[274] This represents asymmetrical conflicts and 4GW at their best, pitting unseen and

---

[268] Bowden, *Killing Pablo*, 253-272.

[269] Kenney, *Pablo to Osama*, 25-47.

[270] Ibid., 33.

[271] Scott H. Decker and Margaret Townsend Chapman, *Drug Smugglers on Drug Smuggling: Lessons from the Inside* (Philadelphia, Temple University Press, 2008), 34.

[272]

[273] Kenney, *Pablo to Osama*, 88-89.

[274] Phil Williams, "Here Be Dragons: Dangerous Spaces and International Security" in eds. Anne L. Clunan and Harold A. Trinkunas, *Ungoverned Spaces: Alternatives to State Authority in an Era of Softened Sovereignty* (Stanford, CA: Stanford University Press/Stanford Security Studies, 2010), 48-49.

mysterious adversaries against international governments whose attention to war remain transitory at best. For private security and protective services personnel, such environments amount to chiseling oneself between bureaucratic political machines and competitively adaptive, covert businesses willing to maim and kill to further their objective.

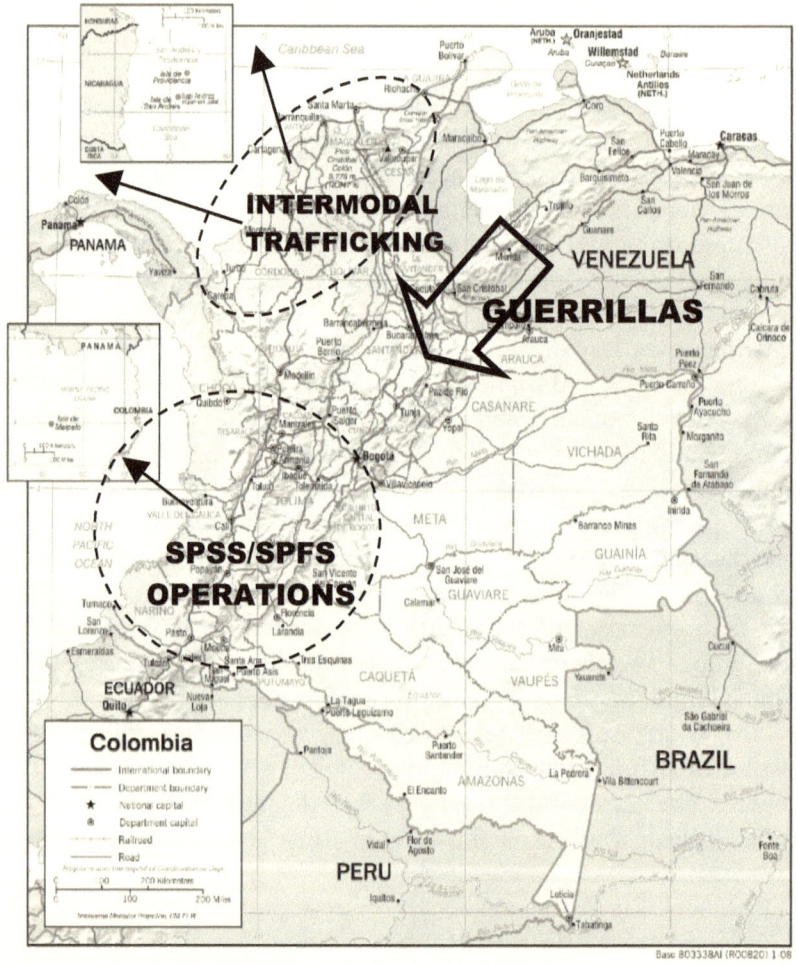

Figure 14. Trafficking Regions of Colombia. Map courtesy of U.S. Central Intelligence Agency.

The primary methods of smuggling today includes human mules, contaminated industrial products, private and commercial aircraft, and self-propelled, semisubmersible (SPSS), self-propelled, fully submersible (SPFS – essentially submarines), towed cargo "torpedoes", and advanced underwater robotic systems. These vehicular smuggling networks are run nearly as effectively as any other legitimate capital enterprise and employ technical assistance from Russians and Chinese, purchasing assistance from Venezuela, and shared *métis* from other criminal and terrorist groups.

The evolution of smuggling technologies adapts to international countermeasures and forces law enforcement agencies into an unsustainable "arms race". For instance, the arrival of Airborne Warning and Control System (AWACS) aircraft caused most narcotics traffickers to shift away from employing aircraft to smuggle narcotics northward.[275] Even today, intelligence reports identifying SPSS and SPFS intercepts have decreased significantly, suggesting that new methods of smuggling may soon appear on the horizon.

For security professionals to counter trafficking operations, they must target either the origin or the terminus of the activity. Once narcotics and other contraband reach the open sea, there remains little hope in locating these shipments. Both U.S. and Latin American authorities, however, attempt impractical measures for countering these threats, seeking to either capture illicit submarines or other maritime vessels on the high seas or disrupt the construction sites manufacturing these illicit vessels.

Evolution of Drug Trafficking

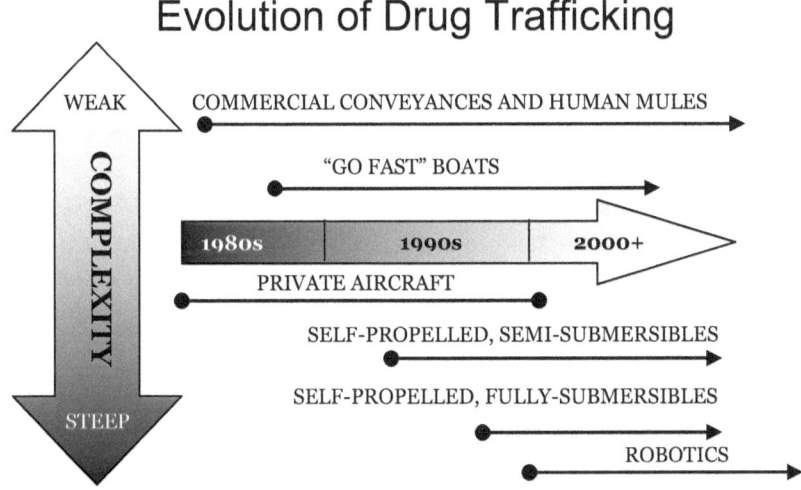

Figure 15. Evolution of Trafficking Technologies. Adapted from R.J. Godlewski, *Targeting Narco-Submarine Networks Through Deep Penetration, Autonomous Maritime Irregular Warfare Units Operating within a Hunter-Killer Role*, Thesis (Charles Town, WV: American Military University, 2013), 38.

[275] Decker and Chapman, *Drug Smugglers*, 80-83.

A significant problem with both U.S. and Colombian efforts to target construction sites for illicit vehicles used in smuggling operations rests with their insertion via extremely loud helicopters or fast river patrol boats.[276] These methods telegraph their presence to narcotics groups well ahead of the counternarcotics forces' arrival, permitting illicit groups to gauge their own actions accordingly.[277] Furthermore, these counternarcotics forces, more often than not, have to be extracted before sunset severely restricting their opportunity to conduct effective operations.[278] A more effective proposal remains to insert small teams of operatives from nondescript cargo vessels plying the waters between North and South America.[279] These tiny clandestine units would spread across the narco-infested jungles and establish relations with disadvantaged persons subjected to the brutality of the trafficking groups in order to gain actionable intelligence without announcing their arrival.[280]

The proposed counternarcotics approach outlined above works on the "out insurgency, the insurgents" philosophy of "he who operates the closest to the local population wins the war". For those professionals engaging within 4GCS, this approach works against piracy as well. That is, modern pirates seek out weak – if not necessarily small – targets and attempt to avoid all confrontation with larger, more powerful adversaries. Maritime officials have declared, "Modern piracy is violent, bloody and ruthless. It is made all the more fearsome because its victims know they are alone and defenseless."[281] Such pirates are not afraid to attack because they understand that even international navies are reluctant to defend the seas.

In the corporate world, the situation becomes even more critical. Historically, working for corporate executives meant "working for cowards".[282] Executives – whether managing large conglomerates or stagnant bureaucracies – tend to acquiesce at the slightest hint of trouble. In 1972, the West German government conspired with the Popular Front for the Liberation of Palestine (PFLP) to stage a phony hijacking of a

---

[276] R.J. Godlewski. *Targeting Narco-Submarine Networks Through Deep Penetration, Autonomous Maritime Irregular Warfare Units Operating within a Hunter-Killer Role,* Thesis (Charles Town, WV: American Military University, 2013), 2.,

[277] Ibid.

[278] Ibid., 41.

[279] Ibid., 53-54.

[280] Ibid.

[281] Quoted in Gray, Monday, and Stubblefield, *Maritime Terror*, 11.

[282] Balor, *Mercenary*, 55.

Lufthansa flight in order to release the three captured terrorists involved within the Olympics massacre.[283] Security professionals engaging within 4GW cannot be as capitulatory. To *defend human life* does not allow atrocities to go unpunished.

The argument in this favor comes from the Roman Catholic Church, "...punish malefactors by means of penalties commensurate with the gravity of the crime, not excluding, *in cases of extreme gravity, the death penalty* [emphasis added]."[284] For similar reasons, the Church holds that "...those holding authority have the right to repel by armed force aggressors against the community in their charge."[285] It remains argued that security professionals – particularly those engaging 4GW adversaries – are defending those in their charge, namely the people employed by and benefiting from the company's existence.

Fear works wonders in dealing with thugs. Pablo Escobar, maniacal murderer that he was, *feared* extradition to the United States.[286] Palestinian terrorists feared assassination by Israel's Mossad and often were forced to live underground.[287] Balor offers an alternative tactic, employing a *feared* despot "detested by the local people they oppress" to gain tactical appreciation from these masses: "Take him out. Visibly. Hoist his body in the village square. And, of course, broadcast the fact."[288] Certainly, this represents a novel approach to wining any "hearts and minds" campaign.[289] Probably not one expected of private security forces, but 4GW represents a *war* and not a transient criminal incident.

Pirates – as with narcotics smugglers – *retreat* towards ungoverned spaces, where such illicit activities as arms trafficking aid their cause.[290] Drug trafficking, itself, funds insurgencies and allows for the appearance of warlords.[291] These pirate communities hijack ships whose stores and cargoes provide valuable commodities from paint and rope to televisions and DVDs, and, in the case of larger and better-organized groups, container loads of manufactured merchandise.[292] These confiscated ships, often turned into "Phantoms" through false

---

[283] Klein, *Striking Back*, 125-128.
[284] *Catechism*, #2266.
[285] Ibid.
[286] Bowden, *Killing Pablo*, 50-59.
[287] Klein, *Striking Back*, 133-135.
[288] Balor, *Mercenary*, 216.
[289] Ibid.
[290] Williams, "Here Be Dragons", 49.
[291] Ibid.
[292] Martin N. Murphy, *Small Boats, Weak States, Dirty Money: Piracy and Maritime Terrorism in the Modern World* (New York: Colombia University Press, 2010), 23.

documentation enacted by pirate 'front companies', serve to swell the coffers of terrorists and other transnational criminal organizations.[293]

Figure 16. Pirates, guerrillas, and terrorists congregate in ungoverned locations. © Abdelhamid Kalai - Fotolia.com

While most commercial shipping companies have declined to place armed guards aboard even their most massive and expensive ships (pirates are nondiscriminatory when it comes to attacking vessels based upon size), owners of tugboats, barges, dredgers, and towed oil rigs in South East Asia have "taken matters into their own hands" and hire private security companies (PSC) to supply armed guards or escort vessels.[294] Clearly, this suggests that vessel operators lack confidence in either indigenous naval or law enforcement agencies coming to their aid when attacked. These smaller operators intimately understand the implications of kidnapping (often for multimillion-dollar ransoms) and murder. Somali pirates, for instance, have been known to hold dozens of vessels and more than 300 crewmembers within their kidnap-for-profit schemes.[295]

Where maritime operations mesh with 4GCS opportunities is through the realization that "the proposals to tame piracy...never seem to touch...the land-based financiers, bankers, spokesmen, support groups, and maritime spy groups that make the actual attacks both possible and

---

[293] Ibid., 24.
[294] Ibid., 36.
[295] Gray, Monday, and Stubblefield, *Maritime Terror*, 9.

profitable."[296] One is left wondering whether Balor's original idea about taking out local despots for "hearts and minds" psychological operations would benefit anti-piracy forces. Certainly, office-bound bankers and financiers would think twice about supporting atrocities if he or she believed that their own lives were in the sights of some private and clandestine tactical unit.

4GCS UNITS	4GW Facet	TERRORISTS
"We can strike where we want when we want – and nobody can stop us."[297]	**Martial**	"*We have the right, to kill 4 million Americans – 2 million of them children – and to exile twice as many and wound and cripple hundreds of thousands.*"[298]
"Love toward oneself remains a fundamental principle of morality. Therefore it is legitimate to insist on respect for one's own right to life. Someone who defends his life is not guilty of murder even if the is forced to deal his aggressor a lethal blow..."[299]	**Religious**	"CHARACTERISTICS OF ASSASSINATION OPERATIONS: Deterring anyone who fights against God and His prophet...It is imperative when designating a target to highlight the latter's crimes and enmity toward Islam and Muslims..."[300]
"Each state...should be able to manage its own political and economic affairs without interference from outside..."[301]	**Political**	"Unless you want to use our music to attack our politics as the governor of Oregon did to drain support away from demonstration against the AmeriKKKan [sic] Legion...Don't let the pigs separate our culture from our politics."[302]
"Frankly, there are no express elevators to the top in financial wealth building – just a long flight of steps."[303]	**Economical**	"One smuggler discussed the profit that could be made with heroin."[304]

[296] Ibid., 8.

[297] Balor, *Mercenary*, 225.

[298] Graham Allison, *Nuclear Terrorism: The Ultimate Preventable Catastrophe* (New York: Times Books, 2004), 12.

[299] *Catechism,* #2264,

[300] Cigar, *Al-Qa'ida's Doctrine*, 142.

[301] Quote in Kegley, R. and Wittkopf, *World Politics*, 124.

[302] Abbie Hoffman in *Mini-Manual of the Urban Guerrilla Warfare by Carlos Marighella* (n.d., booklet ostensibly printed by the Black Panthers and/or The Weathermen terrorist groups ~ Wisconsin circa 1970), 6.

[303] Gary Keller with Dave Jenks and Jay Papasan, *The Millionaire Real Estate Investor* (New York: McGraw-Hill, 2005), 9.

Table 4. Priorities in 4GW.

During the hunt for Pablo Escobar, the paramilitary unit *Los Pepes* (*Perseguidos por Pablo Escobar* – People Persecuted by Pablo Escobar) targeted his finance and legal network to great effect.[305] Without bankers, lawyers, and support personnel, *any* organization – legitimate or otherwise – collapses under the weight of its own responsibilities. Targeting pirates and their safe havens must be conducted with the same ruthless brutality, otherwise the terrorists and their support networks will continue to flourish as taxpayer-funded services diminish and nation-states stick to targeting "known personalities" such as one another. Maritime Irregular Warfare (MIW) should be *the* source of income for extended 4GCS operations, if only businesses and other institutions would take protective service responsibilities more seriously.

POINTS TO CONSIDER

- Piracy and narcotics trafficking represent two multibillion-dollar industries that will not die out without a fight. Unfortunately, international militaries and law enforcement agencies do not possess the resources necessary to protect every company's personnel and assets, even within their resident countries. It is time that private security fights back.

- Pirates have successfully hijacked few, if any, armed commercial vessels. Arming ships, however, need not include firearms. Active Denial Systems (ADS) can keep marauders at bay or, possibly, disable them within the confines of superstructure passageways (think of the ending to 1951's *The Thing from another World*). Creativity remains humanity's most powerful weapon.

- As proven in Sri Lanka's civil war, terrorists possess actual navies. Security forces should too.

- Surrender is most emphatically *not* an option. Bound and gagged targets are easy to shoot. Moving ones, – especially those that shoot back – are more difficult to take down.

---

[304] Decker and Chapman, *Drug Smugglers*, 57.
[305] Bowden, *Killing Pablo*, 191-193.

EXECUTIVE PROTECTION SCENARIO

Hollywood and the music industry have presented the world with a 'worst case' depiction of executive protection professionals (EPP). On the one hand, we have those big, burly individuals that appear more akin to your stereotypical barroom bouncer than legitimate protective services professionals do. Towards the opposite end of the spectrum, we have examples that just *ooze* security detail. These are the individuals dressed in dark suits, wearing dark sunglasses, and constantly fingering an ear bud while talking into their sleeve. These examples draw attention to themselves and, by extension, to the principal under protection.

Unless protective services personnel fit in with the local environment, they signal novelty and this individuality warrants a closer examination. Consider, for instance, a role as a tabloid journalist in Beverley Hills, California. While eating dinner at a swank restaurant, you observe a tall individual directed towards the door by a quartet of muscular men marching along in a square formation wearing the aforementioned dark suits and sunglasses. You, representing the astute "big story" journalist, naturally assume that the protected individual is *important* and, perhaps, suitable for a feature that will aid sales of your checkout lane tabloid. Whether this individual represents an entertainer, an athlete, or a prominent executive or politician matters very little. He *is* important and, therefore, in your eyes, ripe for the pickings. What just happened was that *someone* was targeted for surveillance and inconvenience.

Had the four bodyguards and their principal been dressed in "Casual Friday" attire, a bit relaxed in their formation, and even, perhaps, engaged in mild colloquial conversation, then you, the journalist, may have dismissed the quintet as nothing more extraordinary than a bunch of friends anticipating the evening golf match. This thought would, very likely, be enforced had the principal been accompanied by one or two individuals instead of four. This brief example illustrates the concerns of both appearance and mannerism within the highly complex field of executive protection.

In 4GW, executives come under threat from individual seeking to promote – or target – particular religious, political, and economic beliefs. Whether your principal represents a Jew targeted by Islamists, a Roman Catholic targeted by pro-abortion groups, or an abused housewife targeted by a tyrannical ex-husband, your perception of threats must cover the full spectrum of asymmetrical conflict. The key here remains *perception* – accurate, thoughtful, and insightful reflection upon a particular individual, object, or situation. That is, one must be able to gaze upon a conflicting sea of individuals, personalities, occupations, and situations and discriminate threats from non-threats with little disruption to his or her consciousness.

This is most assuredly not an easy task to accomplish, even for the practiced professional. Executives and other protected individuals rarely remain at home, isolated from crowds, and engage solely within Internet commerce. Instead, he or she goes to "where the action is". In other words, just as paramedics rush to the scene of an accident or soldiers rush into combat, executives and other prominent individuals rush toward various responsibilities and through various schedules. Sometimes, even, this expedient behavior encroaches upon being rash. All of this illustrates why not just "anyone" can serve within EPP. Nor does it allow for "industry certification" automatically declaring an individual versed in asymmetrical warfare.

The reality of 4GW remains that *anything* can occur, at *any time*, and result within *any situation*, presenting a multitude of considerations, simulations, and dismissals for the security professional to evaluate. Each threat or situation or event must be addressed along martial (is it deadly?), religious (is it fanatical?), political (is it expedient?), and economical (is it profitable?) lines. Each segment of life requires its own solution and necessarily affects all others. For instance, is the attack against your client because he is Jewish and therefore an enemy of Islam? Or is it because she is a Jew and therefore discriminated against by someone who feels that Jews are greedy and selfish? Perhaps, even though your client may, in fact, be Jewish, the attack is along political lines and he or she represents a proud Conservative or Progressive.

While your function remains to protect your charge against *all* attacks, each of the above examples illustrates how *particular* situations can lead to specific threats. Fostering perception permits 4GCS professionals to categorize and analyze threats against situations and individuals against events. With time, the professional can segregate his or her operations, methods, equipment, tactics, and expectations. The world of 4GW remains fluid and so, too, must executive protection.

Table 5. Representative scenarios in 4GW Executive Protection.

4GW Facet	Group 1	Group 2
Martial	A narco-trafficker attacks a crowded banquet hall because the owner seeks to improve the conditions of the inner city.	An active shooter penetrates a corporate retreat seeking to kill as many executives as possible.
Religious	A pro-abortion or gay rights supporter attacks a Roman Catholic columnist based upon his stance against killing the unborn and same-sex marriages.	A Progressive activist promoting "Separation of Church and State" plans to disrupt business at a Christian-owned restaurant.
Political	A Palestinian terrorist attacks a Jewish athlete because of the latter's "Zionist" attitudes.	Russian football fans seeking Crimean secession target a Ukrainian athlete.
Economical	An Occupy Wall Street operative targets a prominent financial executive.	A recently laid off employee targets a human resource specialist.

The above table suggest ways in which 4GW applies within the modern world. The typical EPP may not separate threats – any threat against a principal must be dealt with *as a threat* – but various martial, religious, political, and economic indicators intensify certain individuals. For example, in Group 2, the conflict between soccer teams may have very little to do with economics. On the other hand, conflicts between, say, Poles and Russians must consider the religious element, as Poles remain overwhelmingly Roman Catholic whereas Russians are Orthodox. In Group 1, attacks against Jews may be either political or religious in nature and, very likely both.

Unlike other aspects of 4GW, which could be considered as groups or ideas against other groups and ideas, executive protection exists fundamentally as individuals threatened by other individuals. The individual attack could represent poisoning, shooting, vehicular assault, bombing, kidnapping, or blackmail, but the actual intent itself rests with isolating *a particular individual* from his or her safety zone.

Figure 17. An accident? © Duncan Noakes - Fotolia.com

Even the most seemingly minor event must be carefully scrutinized for ulterior motives, even if the EPP partook of the event. In 4GW, the most popular tactic in kidnappings or even murder remains ambushes. Al-Qaeda, as but one prominent 4GW group, bears implicit instructions for both attacking *and* protecting motorcades.[306] Their detailed diagrams indicate analysis of presidential or national motorcade policies.[307] If this is, indeed, the case, then so much more prepared must be the EPP protecting a singular individual. Most protective services professionals, unfortunately, cannot match the strengths and resources of groups such as al-Qaeda (which are, after all, supported immeasurably by totalitarian nations such as Iran, Saudi Arabia, and North Korea).

The question then becomes how EP teams can employ 4GW as a force-multiplier to level the field as much as possible. Several actions can increase the likelihood of protecting executives and other prominent individuals (not to mention families and friends of 4GCS personnel). These actions are broad and, as always, open to interpretation and innovation.

---

[306] Cigar, *Al-Qa'ida's Doctrine*, 149-155.
[307] Ibid., 150-155.

- **Martial Appreciation**. Garret Machine establishes the mood when he writes, "…you are a *security warrior*" and elaborates on the mentality that professionals must adopt before he or she is placed into a situation where lives are on the line.[308] With Iran seeking nuclear weapons, North Korea consistently abducting people from abroad, Syria gassing its citizens, and Russia pulling a page from Nazi Germany[309] in order to invade Ukraine, *no one* can escape the need to develop a tactical mentality. Forrest Morgan discusses why waitresses, bricklayers, doctors, and other persons "neither born into a warrior heritage nor involved in the profession of arms" would need to consider themselves today as warriors.[310] His contention remains that warriors appreciate the concept of honor and follow ethical standards long since abandoned by society.[311] They remain the ones who *defend* the defenseless. Remember, radical Islamists and narco-traffickers are *not fanatical* individuals. They simply believe in what they are doing. In today's ultra-facetious society, devotion to life may seem ridiculous, but if security professionals do not fight for life, then *who* will? Martial appreciation of life simply means that human lives are worth fighting for and this attitude just may provide enough stamina to endure the "long war".

- **Religious Empowerment.** "Nobody may be forced to act against his convictions, nor is anyone to be restrained from acting in accordance with his conscience in religious matters in private or in public, alone or in association with others, within due limits."[312] In this brief statement, protective services professionals can activate several powerful "tools" necessary to protect human lives. Religious faith provides an individual with the substance to avoid compromising his or her conscience. If one believes in God, for instance, they are unlikely to compromise core values for transitory benefits. In the context of an *eternal* afterlife, a mere 50 or 100 years on earth pales in comparison. The stronger the faith,

---

[308] Machine, *Security Warrior*, 117.

[309] Vladimir Putin claims to be aiding ethnic Russians in southern Ukraine and the Crimea. Adolf Hitler as a pretext in invading Austria and Czechoslovakia used the same argument. Hitler further sent agents into Poland to instigate reasons for invading that neighbor. Putin appears to have done the same – appropriately, right after the 2014 Olympics in Sochi closed when the world could not protest.

[310] Morgan, *Martial Way*, 25-26.

[311] Ibid., 26.

[312] Quote in *Catechism*, #2106.

therefore, the less likely that politicians, criminals, educators, and other influencers are able to chip away at an individual's character. Furthermore, religious faith is not meant to be restrained in public despite modern society's fascination with secularism. These beliefs – in public – serve as a reminder to threatening individuals that the protective services professional is not constrained in his or her duty to protect lives *at any cost*. Call it simple psychological warfare, if you will, but "God" does cause fear in individuals – providing that the believer does not blink.

- *Political Minefields.* Politics, generally, represents the antithesis of religious devotion. What is "sometimes" considered a calling to service invariably ends up as a means to discriminate against others under the cloak of personal profit. Politicians, as already represented the case of West German authorities staging a hijacked airliner as a ploy to send the three surviving Munich murders home, will abandon his or her core beliefs just for political survival. In fact, the press, other politicians, and many members of the public often ostracize politicians that retain honesty in their dealings. Practitioners of 4GCS, however, employ politics as an offensive weapon. They turn the psychological tables against political individuals because the latter remain susceptible to "the vote". Even local municipal politicians are extremely concerned about acquiring votes, particularly during relatively frequent election cycles. Bad publicity turns actors into superstars, but such notoriety often defeats political leaders. EP professionals need to be constantly aware of the political implications afforded by every action. Case in point, the prospects of extradition ultimately flushed Pablo Escobar out into the public where he was ultimately killed.

- *Raw, Economic Persuasion*. To reiterate the old adage, money indeed talks. In modern society – where camping out on the plains and bartering goods with a mere handshake no longer qualify as civility – currency trumps both religion and politics and powers martial aggression and defense. Without capital investments, few are able to achieve his or her goals. Furthermore, those within a burgeoning entitlement society are often at the whim of those who control the purse strings. 4GCS can use this to affect his or her trade.

We can now place this arsenal of 4GW into EPP hands, employing each element individually and in groups to protect principals and other individuals. In the context of globalization and the increasing availability of cellular telephones, high-speed wireless data connections, and digital cameras, illicit society has become something of a universal insurgency. In this regard, Poole's assertion that 4GW counterinsurgency warrants a paradigm shift in security operations applies equally to protective services within the private sector.[313] His recognition that if insurgents (Maoist or otherwise) can swim through a sea of people, then that population needs to befriended by security forces in order to defeat the aggressors.[314]

Since protected individuals are often on the move – necessitating protective details as movement diminishes security – then there always remains three points of consideration: origin, presence, and terminus. As these names suggest, these terms represent the beginning of one's journey, their location at any particular moment, and, finally, wherever they cease moving, respectively. Whether one's movements entail several hours' of a journey or merely a few seconds, their path occupies this progression. Accordingly, such a journey can only exist for a few hours at best since once a person ceases to move, they begin the origin-presence-terminus journey all over again.

Consider the path of a marathon runner versus a busy executive within a corporate campus setting. The athlete begins his or her run at the origin – the starting line and the terminus represents, naturally, the finish line. His or her presence, however, depends upon *time*. If it takes them three hours to complete a race and the marathon begins at 9 A.M., then at 10:15 A.M., 11:32 A.M. and 11: 59 A.M. they are always presence along the course, but at different locations. Conversely, the executive's journeys are much shorter, but consist of more considerations. His or her movement through the campus and through the individual buildings represents a myriad of shorter and longer walks.

If the workday begins at 7:00 A.M., their first origin may very well represent the front door of his or her home terminating at the office desk. Another origin may begin at 9:02 A.M. finding them terminating at marketing on the seventh floor. After a brief ten-minute chat, the executive may walk around several yards of grounds to reach a noon meeting located in Building 107. Their terminus – and, thus, presence – in that building may last for several hours depending upon the importance of the meeting. Once they move, the process begins anew.

---

[313] Poole, *Tequila*, 181.
[314] Ibid., 181-182.

Figure 18. Counter-personnel threats are growing in sophistication. © hurricane - Fotolia.com

To protect individuals, protective services details must establish *advances* to reconnoiter each location planned or perceived to become part of either the terminus of the principal's motions or likely to represent his or her presence during any *specific point* in the future. In EP work, there is no such thing as "the shortest distance between two points is a straight line" no matter how desirous that statement may appear. In wading through a "universal insurgency" nothing can be guaranteed – even a walk across the office may be disrupted by any number of occurrences. Therefore, while an individual within a protective detail keeps his or eyes on the principal and potential threats within the immediate vicinity, their mind is eternally considering various potentialities along the expected route. A typical day in the life of a busy executive could find EP personnel struggling with literally dozens of origin-presence-terminus scenarios, only to start the process seven days a week.

Figure 19. When executive protection goes bad... © Martin Spurny - Fotolia.com

Eventually, especially within corporate operations, executives travel to locations foreign (though not necessarily international) to his or her routine. This places the principal in "virgin territory" where threats previously encountered may not represent the threats that actually exist. This further means that the principal's EP detachment must reconnoiter the location – especially if it represents a terminus – before the executive reaches the area. 4GW, being what it is, requires the participation of indigenous personnel to effectively plan travel and lodging within that city. Simply showing up and asking questions is not very practical; even relatively civilized people tend to be xenophobic if languages, dialects, clothing, and mannerisms appear unusual.

You, as an advance scout, will have two things going for your mission. First, even in chaotic Third World locations where all hell seems to be breaking loose, public services and even airline flights continue operating as if normal. This aids in the fact that local citizens will not only bear up-to-date information, but that even in the dire case of societal collapse, the prospects for getting an executive out of harms' way remain good. The second thing going for you rests with humanity's natural inclination (at least in most parts of the world) to form bonds with visitors – providing that such visitors are not perceived as invaders. A solitary individual or very small group providing reconnaissance of a location can benefit from making critical alliances with retail clerks, hotel managers, and, especially, local law enforcement and security companies.

Gratuities provided to merchants work as well as economic promises made to politicians. A contribution to local clergy also opens many doors to cooperative persons, many of whom may share political and/or economic interests in having a "wealthy corporation" come into town to save them from whatever institution is creating their hardships. For this scenario to even possess a chance of working, EP advance teams must treat any indigenous person as an equal and not have them believe that the visiting security team is trampling over them as if an onslaught from your stereotypical "superpower".[315]

EP advance teams must operate as "information curators", absorbing all available information and cultivating any available association to protect their charge. The implications of 4GCS remain a psychological duel between adversaries, each devoting literal blood to the cause of survival. Indigenous persons routinely support the side that best represents the one that he or she does not want to anger. This respect can be magnified exponentially with some kindness and compassion when backed by authoritative power and the skill to employ it. As, above all else, a psychological operation, 4GCS builds upon both reputation and experience, permitting individual far removed from company operations to anticipate the arrival of an executive force. Sometimes, conversely, this reputation appears without forewarning as EP teams versed in 4GW assume a preconditioning that allows individual members to act within particular cultures without conscious prodding.

In the 1998 action movie, *Ronin*, Robert DeNiro's character "Sam" pulls a masterful feint upon a personal protection detail. First, under the ruse of a vacationing couple, Sam asks a hotel guest to photograph him and his "wife" Deirdre. At first, Sam shows the guest how to use the camera, which, in actuality, permits Sam to photograph the security detail (by refraining from looking *through* the camera, no one should notice anything

---

[315] Ibid., 182.

unusual). After "explaining" the camera's operation to the guest, Sam then asks him to photograph the couple with the backdrop of Nice, France's palm trees in the distance. This panorama covers the presence of the security detail as they move towards their automobiles, during which Sam asks the recruited photographer to take shots of Deirdre alone. At this time, Sam walks outside to a cart of luggage and tilts a heavy metal sign against the cart and retreats to the hotel, stopping briefly to tip a bellhop to hurry the bags into the building.

Knowing what is about to happen, Sam then offers to photograph the guest with Deirdre and quickly diverts to photographing the security detail when the sign hits the pavement as the hotel staff moves the cart. Believing the sound to represent possible gunfire, the security detail's response rests conveniently photographed for subsequent study by Sam's team of hired gunmen. This scene, while great for entertainment and, perhaps, analysis by real security details, leaves much to be critical of nevertheless. Why did the security detail parade their principle (whose briefcase handcuffed to his wrist suggested that he was aware of his being a target) past a cart full of luggage, any one of which could have contained an explosive device.

With several guards – and relatively little commotion – present, why did someone *not* notice Sam's actions with the heavy sign only a few feet away? Finally, with *numerous* security professionals available, enough to fill several automobiles, why was there not anyone *outside* the immediate perimeter that could have noticed the events that permitted Sam's actions? Although no Hollywood movie remains entirely realistic, *Ronin* offers an opportunity to gauge traditional protective services against the 4GCS model.

In 4GCS, protective details cannot exclusively drag their charge into locations under the assumption that they provide a security 'bubble' around the principal. Too many factors conspire to collapse that bubble with little or no warning. Preferably, large security units should be able to create a safe zone that allows a principal to move *into* (and out of) before events collapse around the executive. This is accomplished by a strong intelligence effort (aided immensely with today's cyber capabilities) coupled simultaneously with an effective ground "hearts and minds" campaign, ideally one initiated by corporate planners *long* before executives begin moving into virgin territory.

The realities of 4GW dictate that whichever side presents the most power *and* finesse will succeed in swaying indigenous populations. When these populations rest within ethnically bound or tribally based areas, Western corporations will always remain at a decided disadvantage as these cultures align themselves with people more attractive to his or her expectations. Advanced 4GCS can level this discrepancy by countering with corporate advantages implemented by an effective security department. After all, "a sleeping Rottweiler commands more respect than a barking Chihuahua."[316] Fourth-generation (and dimension) corporate security provides the opportunity to command respect at a cost more advantageous than reactionary measures based upon traditional security failures.

POINTS TO CONSIDER

- Without a *martial* approach to executive protection, religious, political, and economic efforts will surrender to those possessing more aggression.

- Possessing a strong martial capability does not absolve a company from maximize efforts to gain the respect of indigenous cultures through social programs, education, and capital development.

- Negotiation without strength represents little more than unconditional surrender.

- *Nobody* should value the life of your principal more than you and his immediate family.

- Consider and question *everything*.

- Laws only hold value in court.

- "Legitimate defense is a *grave duty for whoever is responsible for the lives of others* or the common good [emphasis added]." *Catechism*, #2321

---

[316] Memorandum for the record, R.J. Godlewski.

SELECTED BIBLIOGRAPHY

109th United States Congress. *Hearing Before the Subcommittee on Immigration, Border Security, And Claims of the Committee on the Judiciary House of Representatives.* Serial No. 109-58, Washington: U.S. Government Printing Office, 2005.

AbuKhalil, As'ad. "Arab-Israeli Conflict." In *The Middle East*, by CQ Press, 13-78. Washington: CQ Press, 2005.

Akhavan, Jacqueline. *The Chemistry of Explosives.* Second Edition. Cambridge: Royal Society of Chemistry, 2006.

Aloise, Gene, interview by the Federal Workforce, and the District of Columbia, Committee on Homeland Security and Governmental Affairs, U.S. Senate Subcommittee on Oversight of Government Management. *COMBATING NUCLEAR TERRORISM: Federal Efforts to Respond to Nuclear and Radiological Threats and to Protect Key Emergency Response Facilities Could Be Strengthened.* U.S. Government Accountability Office, (15 November 2007).

al-Qaeda. "Declaration of Jihad (Holy War) Against the Country's Tyrants, Military Series."

Alterman, Jon B. *The Real Shi'a-Sunni Conflict.* Washington: Center for Strategic and International Studies, 2007.

Andrew, Christopher. *For the President's Eyes Only: Secret Intelligence and the American Presidency from Washington to Bush.* New York: Harper Collins, 1995.

Andrew, Christopher, and Vasili Mitrokhin. *The Sword and the Shield: The Mitrokhin Archive and the Secret History of the KGB.* New York: Basic Books, 1999.

Argonne National Laboratory. *Radiological Disperal Device (RDD).* Human Health Fact Sheet, Chicago: Argonne National Laboratory, 2005.

Arias, Enrique Desmond. "Understanding Criminal Networks, Political Order, and Politics in Latin America." In *Ungoverned Spaces: Alternatives to State Authority in an Era of Softened Sovereignty,* edited by Anne L. Clunan and Harold A. Trinkunas, 115-135. Stanford, CA: Stanford Security Studies/Stanford University Press, 2010.

Armstrong, Karen. *A History of God: The 4,000-Year Quest of Judaism, Christianity, and Islam.* New York: Ballantine Books, 1993.

Army, United States. *TM 31-210 Improvised Munitions Handbook.* Washington: Department of the Army, 1969.

Aslan, Reza. *No god but God: The Origins, Evolution, and Future of Islam.* New York: Random House, 2006.

Baer, Robert. "Politics: GQ." *GQ Magazine Web site.* April 2010. http://www.gq.com/news-politics/politics/201004/dagger-to-the-cia (accessed April 17, 2010).

—. *See No Evil: The True Story of a Ground Soldier in the CIA's War on Terrorism.* New York: Three Rivers Press, 2002.

Balor, Paul. *Manual of the Mercenary Soldier.* Boulder: Paladin Press, 1988.

Beason, Doug. *The E-Bomb: How America's New Directed Energy Weapons Will Change the Way Future Wars Will Be Fought.* Cambridge, MA: Da Capo Press, 2005.

Bejtlich, Richard. "Cooking the Cuckoo's Egg." Vers. 1.0. *Tao Security Website.* 2 February 2011. http://www.taosecurity.com/bejtlich_doj_cooking_06feb11a.pdf (accessed December 13, 2012).

Belfield, Richard. *The Assassination Business: A history of state-sponsored murder.* New York: Carroll & Graf Publishers, 2005.

Benson, Ragnar. *Gunrunning for Fun & Profit.* Boulder: Paladin Press, 1986.

Bergman, Ronen. "Hezbollah and the Lebanon Dilemma." *Wall Street Journal (Eastern edition)*, 5 August 2010: A17.

Berkowitz, Bruce D. "The Logic of Covert Action." *The National Interest*, 1998.

Bernstein, Paul I. *Weapons of Mass Destruction: A Primer*. Technical Instruction, Advanced Systems and Concepts Office, Washington: Defense Threat Reduction Agency, 2006.

Biddle, Stephen, and Jeffrey A. Friedman. *THE 2006 LEBANON CAMPAIGN AND THE FUTURE OF WARFARE: Implications for Army and Defense Policy*. Carlisle, PA: Strategic Studies Institute, 2008.

Black, Ian, and Benny Morris. *Israel's Secret Wars: A History of Israel's Intelligence Services*. New York: Grove Press, 1991.

Bodansky, Yossef. *Chechen Jihad: Al-Qaeda's Training Ground and the Next Wave of Terror*. New York: Harper, 2007.

—. "CHECHNYA: The Mujahedin Factor."

—. *TERROR! The inside story of the terrorist conspiracy in America*. SPI Books, 1994.

Bowden, Mark. *Killing Pablo: The Hunt for the World's Greatest Outlaw*. New York: Penguin Books, 2001.

Bradley, Gabriel. "Honor, Not Law: Rules of engagement are only a small part of battlefield discipline." *Armed Forces Journal*, March 2012: 16-21,31.

Brands, Hal. *Crime, Violence, and the Crisis in Guatemala: A Case Study in the Erosion of the State*. Strategic Study, Carlisle: Strategic Studies Institute, 2010.

—. *Dealing with Political Ferment in Latin America: the Populist Revival, the Emergence of the Center, and Implication for U.S. Policy*. Carlisle, PA: Strategic Studies Institute, 2009.

Brands, Hal. *Mexico's Narco-Insurgency and U.S. Counterdrug Policy*. Strategic Study, Carlisle, PA: Strategic Studies Institute, 2009.

Brodarick, Ann Marie. "High Seas, High Stakes: Jurisdiction over Stateless Vessels and an Excess of Congressional Power Under the Drug Trafficking Vessel Interdiction Act." *University of Miami Law Review* 67 (2012): 255-276.

Bullock, Alan. *Hitler and Stalin: Parallel Lives.* New York: Vintage, 1993.

Byman, Daniel. *Deadly Connections: States that Sponsor Terrorism.* New York: Cambridge University Press, 2005.

Celeski, Joseph D. *Hunter-Killer Teams: Attacking Enemy Safe Havens.* Report 10-1, Hurlburt Field, FL: Joint Special Operations University, 2010.

Cherkashin, Victor, and Gregory Feifer. *Spy Handler: Memoir of a KGB Officer.* New York: Basic Books, 2005.

Chinn, Ko-lin. *Chinatown Gangs: Extortion, Enterprise, & Ethnicity.* New York: Oxford University Press, 1996.

Clark, Robert M. *Intelligence Analysis: A target-centric approach.* Washington: CQ Press, 2007.

Clarke, Richard A., and Robert K. Knake. *Cyber War: The Next Threat to National Security and What to Do about It.* New York: Harper Collins/Ecco, 2010.

Clausewitz, Carl von. *On War.* Translated by Michael Howard and Peter Paret. Princeton: Princeton University Press, 1984.

Coll, Steve. *Ghost Wars: The Secret History of the CIA, Afghanistan, and Bin Laden, from the Soviet Invasion to Steptember 10, 2001.* New York: Penguin Books, 2004.

Colling, Russell L., and Tony W. York. *Hospital and Healtchare Security.* 5th Edition. Burlington, MA: Elsevier, 2010.

Couch, Dick. *A Tactical Ethic: Moral Conduct in the Insurgent Battlespace.* Annapolis, MD: Naval Institute Press, 2010.

Cox, Robert. "Total Terrorism: Argentina, 1969 to 1979." In *Terrorism, Legitimacy, and Power*, by Martha Crenshaw, 124-142. Middletown, CT: Wesleyan, 1983.

Cragin, Kim, and Bruce Hoffman. *Arms Trafficking and Colombia.* Santa Monica, CA: RAND Corporation, 2003.

Crawford, George A. *Manhunting: Counter-Network Organization for Irregular Warfare*. JSOU Report 09-7, Hurlbert Field: Joint Special Operations University, 2009.

Cutler, Thomas J. *Brown Water, Black Berets*. Annapolis, MD: Naval Institute Press, 1988.

Cwiek, Mark A. *America after 9/11*. Vol. I, chap. 2 in *Community Preparedness and Response to Terrorism: The Terrorist Threat and Community Response*, edited by Gerald R. Ledlow, James A. Johnson and Walter J. Jones, 7-21. Westport, Connecticut: Praeger, 2005.

Dashti, Ali. "Twenty Three Years: A study of the Prophetic Career of Mohammad." 1994.

Dauber, Cori I. *YouTube War: Fighting in a World of Cameras in every Cell Phone and Photoshop on every Computer*. Carlisle, PA: Strategic Studies Institute, 2009.

Davis, Anthony M. *Terrorism and the Maritime Transportation System: Are We on a Collision Course?* Livermore, CA: WingSpan Press, 2008.

De Andreis, Marco, and Francesco Calogero. *The Soviet Nuclear Weapon Legacy*. New York: SIPRI/Oxford University Press, 1995.

de Wijze, Stephen. "Targeted killing: a 'dirty hands' analysis." *Contemporary Politics* 15, no. 3 (September 2009): 305-320.

Decker, Scott H., and Margaret Townsend Chapman. *Drug Smugglers on Drug Smuggling: Lessons from the Inside*. Philadelphia: Temple University Press, 2008.

Department of the Army. *FM 3-05.30 PSYCHOLOGICAL OPERATIONS*. Field Manual, Washington: United States Government, 2005.

Department of the Army, Headquarters. *FM 3-55.93 Long-Range Surveillance Unit Operations*. Washington: United States Government, 2009.

Dobson, Christopher, and Ronald Payne. *Counterattack: The West's battle against the terrorists*. New York: Facts on File, Inc., 1982.

Dunigan, Molly, Dick Hoffman, Peter Chalk, Brian Nichiporuk, and Paul Deluca. *Characterizing and Exploring the Implications of Maritime Irregular Warfare*. Santa Monica, CA: RAND Corporation, 2012.

Durant, Will. *The Age of Faith*. New York: Simon and Schuster, 1950.

Ehrenfeld, Rachel. *Funding Evil: How Terrorism is Financed -- and How to Stop it*. Chicago: Bonus Books, 2003.

Ellis, John W. *Police Analysis and Planning for Homicide Bombings: Prevention, Defense, and Response*. Springfield, IL: Charles C. Thomas Publisher, Ltd., 2007.

Ellis, R. Evan. *China-Latin America Military Engagement: Good Will, Good Business, and Strategic Position*. Carlisle, PA: Strategic Studies Institute, 2011.

Emerson, Steven. *American Jihad: The Terrorists Living Amongst Us*. New York: The Free Press, 2002.

England, James W. *Long-Range Patrol Operations: Reconnaissance, Combat, and Special Operations*. Boulder: Paladin Press, 1987.

Eshel, David. "Defeating IEDs." *The Journal of Electronic Defense*, December 2007: 38-42.

Fainaru, Steve. *Big Boy Rules: America's Mercenaries Fighting in Iraq*. Philadelphia: Da Capo Press, 2008.

Fay, John J. *Contemporary security management*. Third. Burlington, MA: Buttersworth-Heinemann, 2011.

Ferguson, Charles D., and William C. Potter. *Improvised Nuclear Devices and Nuclear Terrorism*. Research Paper, Stockholm: The Weapons of Mass Destruction Commission, 2004.

Fishel, John T., and Max G. Manwaring. *Uncomfortable Wars Revisited*. Norman, OK: University of Oklahoma Press, 2006.

Flanigan, Shawn Teresa, and Mounah Abdel-Samad. "Hezbollah's Social Jihad: Nonprofits as Resistance Organizations." *Middle East Policy* XVI, no. 2 (2009): 122-137.

Fowler, Will. *The Special Forces Guide to Escape and Evasion*. New York: Thomas Dunne Books, 2005.

Gabriel, Mark A. *Journey into the Mind of an Islamic Terrorist*. Lake Mary, Florida: Front Line, 2006.

Garner, Robert J. *Ethical Guidelines for Military Covert Operations.* USAWC Military Studies Program Paper, Carlisle Barracks, Pennsylvania: U.S. Army War College, 1990.

Gerges, Fawaz. *Journey of the Jihadist: Inside Muslim Militancy.* Orlando: Harcourt, 2006.

Gilbert, Adrian. *Sniper: One on One: The World of Combat Sniping.* London: Sidgwick & Jackson, 1994.

Glazebrook, Jerry, and Nick Nicholson. *Executive Protection Specialist Handbook.* Second Edition. Shawnee Mission, Kansas: Varro Press, 2003.

Godlewski, R.J. "Cultivating Creativity within Intelligence Analysis." *American Intelligence Journal* 25, no. 2 (2008): 85-87.

Godlewski, R.J. "Financial Counterintelligence: Fractioning the Lifeblood of Asymmetrical Warfare." *American Intelligence Journal* 29, no. 2 (2011): 24-33.

Godlewski, R.J. "Human Intelligence: Perceiving an Enemy's Thoughts." *American Intelligence Journal* 27, no. 1 (2009): 29-37.

Godlewski, R.J. "Latte Intelligence: The Divorce of Shock Creativity and Special Information Operations." *American Intelligence Journal* 29, no. 1 (2011): 70-79.

—. *Mini-Manual of the Independent Counterterrorist.* Second. Charleston, SC: CreateSpace Independent Publishing Platform, 2012.

—. *Skills of the Assassin: Understanding the Tactics of the Professional Killer.* Charleston: CreateSpace Independent Publishing Platform, 2012.

Godson, Roy. *Dirty Tricks or Trump Cards: U.S. Cover Action & Counterintelligence.* New Brunsick (U.S.A.): Transaction Publishers, 2008.

Goodrich, Thomas. *Scalp Dance: Indian Warfare on the High Plains 1865-1879.* Mechanicsburg , Pennsylvania: Stackpole Books, 1997.

Gray, Colin S. *Another Bloody Century: Future Warfare.* London: Phoenix, 2006.

Gray, Jim, Mark Monday, and Gary Stubblefield. *Maritime Terror: Protecting Yourself, Your Vessel, and Your Crew against Piracy.* Boulder: Paladin Press, 2011.

Grayson, George W. *La Familia Drug Cartel: Implications for U.S.-Mexican Security*. Carlisle, PA: Strategic Studies Institute, 2010.

Gross, Michael L. *Moral Dilemmas of Modern War: Torture, Assassination, and Blackmail in an Age of Asymmetric Conflict*. New York: Cambridge University Press, 2010.

Grossman, Dave. *On Killing: The Psychological Cost of Learning to Kill in War and Society*. Revised. New York: Back Bay Books, 2009.

Guevara, Che. *Guerrilla Warfare*. New York: Monthly Review Press, 1961.

Hamilton, Scott. "Cyber Threats: We don't know what we don't know." *Armed Forces Journal*, November 2009: 33-34, 41.

Harclerode, Peter. *Fighting Dirty: The Inside Story of Covert Operations from Ho Chi Minh to Osama Bin Laden*. London: Cassell & Company, 2001.

Hayes, Stephen K. *The Ninja and their secret fighting art*. Rutland, VT: Charles E. Tuttle Company, 1981.

Headquarters, Department of the Army. *FM 3-06 Combined Arms Operations in Urban Terrain*. Washington: Department of the Army, 2002.

Heiden, Konrad. *Der Fuehrer: Hitler's rise to power*. Boston: Houghton Mifflin Company, 1944.

Herrington, Stuart A. *Stalking the Vietcong: Inside Operation Phoenix: A Personal Account*. New York: Ballantine Books, 1982.

Herzog, Chaim. *The Arab-Israeli Wars: War and Peace in the Middle East from the War of Independence through Lebanon*. New York: Vintage, 1982.

Heuer Jr., Richards J., and Randolph H. Pherson. *Structured Analytic Techniques For Intelligence Analysis*. Washington: CQ Press, 2011.

Hoffman, Bruce. "A Nasty Business." In *Terrorism and Counterterrorism: Understanding the New Security Environment: Readings and Interpretations*, by Russell D. Howard and Reid L. Sawyer, 402-407. Dubuque, Iowa: McGraw-Hill, 2006.

Hoffman, Frank G. "Mind Maneuvers: The Psychological Element of Counterinsurgency Warfare can be the Most Persuasive." *Armed Forces Journal*, April 2007: 28-32.

Hourani, Albert. *A History of the Arab Peoples*. New York: Warner Books, 1991.

Howard, Russel D. *Intelligence in Denied Areas: New Concepts for a Changing Security Environment*. JSOU Report 07-10, Hurlbert Field: Joint Special Operations University, 2007.

Hristov, Jasmin. "Self-Defense Forces, Warlords, or Criminal Gangs? Towards a New Conceptualization of Paramilitarism in Colombia." *Labour, Capital & Society* 43, no. 2 (2010): 14-56.

Hunter, Thomas B. *Targeted Killing: Self-Defense, Preemption, and the War on Terrorism*. Lexington, KY: BookSurge, 2009.

Hurth, John D. *Combat Tracking Guide*. Mechanicsburg, PA: Stackpole Books, 2012.

Ibrahim, Raymond. *War and Peace -- and Deceit -- in Islam*. Pajamas Media, 2009.

Jaber, Hala. *Hezbollah: Born with a Vengeance*. New York: Columbia University Press, 1997.

Johnson, William R. *Thwarting Enemies at Home and Abroad: How to be a Counterintelligence Officer*. Washington: Georgetown University Press, 2009.

Jones, Adam. "Parainstitutional Violence in Latin America." *Latin American Politics and Society* 46, no. 4 (2004): 127-148.

Jones, Andy, Gerald l Kovacich, and Perry G. Luzwick. *Global Information Warfare: How Businesses, Governments, and Others Achieve Objectives and Attain Competitive Advantages*. New York: Auerbach, 2002.

Jones, Ishmael. *The Human Factor: Inside the CIA's Dysfunctional Intelligence Culture*. New York: Encounter Books, 2010.

Jonsson, Fredrik C. *Maritime Sniper Manual: Precision Fire from Seaborne Platforms*. Boulder: Paladin Press, 2010.

Kahaner, Larry. *AK-47: The weapon that changed the face of war*. Hoboken: John Wiley & Sons, Inc., 2007.

Kahn, David. *Hitler's Spies: German Military Intelligence in World War II*. New York: Collier Books, 1978.

Kan, Paul Rexton. *Drug Intoxicated Irregular Fighters: Complications, Dangers, and Responses*. Carlisle, PA: Strategic Studies Institute, 2008.

—. *Mexico's "Narco-Refugees": The Looming Challenge for U.S. National Security*. Carlisle, PA: Strategic Studies Institute, 2011.

Kay, Christobal. "Reflections on Rual Violence in Latin America." *Third World Quarterly* 22, no. 5 (2001): 741-775.

Kegley Jr., Charles W, and Eugene R. Wittkopf. *World Politics: Trend and Transformation*. Third Edition. New York: St. Marten's, 1989.

Kellner, Tomas, and Francesco Pipitone. "Inside Mexico's Drug War." *World Policy Journal*, 2010: 29-37.

Kenney, Michael. *From Pablo to Osama: Trafficking and Terrorist Networks, Government Bureaucracies, and Competitive Adaptation*. University Park, PA: The Pennsylvania State University Press, 2007.

Kenney, Michael. "The Architecture of Drug Trafficking: Network Forms of Organisation in the Colombian Cocaine Trade." *Global Crime* 8, no. 3 (2007): 233-259.

Kennison, Peter, and Amanda Loumansky. "Shoot to kill -- understanding police use of force in combatting suicide terrorism." *Crime, Law, and Social Change* 47, no. 3 (2007): 151-168.

Kibbe, Jennifer D. "Covert Action and the Pentagon." *Intelligence and National Security*, 2007: 57-74.

Kiernan, Kathleen L. "Counterintelligence and Law Enforcement." In *Vaults, Mirrors, & Masks: Rediscovering U.S. Counterintelligence*, by Jennifer E. Sims and Burton Gerber, 149-171. Washington: Georgetown University Press, 2009.

Klein, Aaron J. *Striking Back: The 1972 Munich Olympics Massacre and Israel's Deadly Response*. New York: Random House, 2007.

Kouzminov, Alexander. *Biological Espionage: Special Operations of the Soviet and Russian Foreign Intelligence Services in the West*. London: Greenhill Books, 2005.

Kovats-Bernat, J. Christopher. "Factional Terror, Paramilitarism and Civil War in Haiti: The View from Port-au-Prince, 1994-2004." *Anthropologia* 48 (2006): 117-139.

Krepinevich, Andrew F. *7 Deadly Scenarios: A Military Futurist Explores War in the Twenty-First Century.* New York: Bantam Books, 2010.

Kushner, Harvey, and Bart Davis. *Holy War on the Home Front: The Secret Islamic Terror Network in the United States.* New York: Sentinel, 2004.

Lambakis, Steven J. "Reconsidering Asymmetric Warfare." *Joint Force Quarterly*, 2004: 102-108.

Lance, Peter. *1000 years for revenge: International terrorism and the FBI -- the untold story.* New York: Regan Books, 2003.

Lanning, Michael Lee. *Inside the LRRPs: Rangers in Vietnam.* New York: Presidio Press, 2006.

Laqueur, Walter. *The Age of Terrorism.* Boston: Little, Brown and Company, 1987.

Lawrence, T.E. *Seven Pillars of Wisdom.* New York: Doubleday, Doran & Company, Inc., 1935.

Lee, Gregory D. *Global Drug Enforcement: Practical Investigative Techniques.* Boca Raton, FL: CRC Press, 2004.

Leebaert, Derek. *To Dare and to Conquer: Special Operations and the Destiny of Nations from Achilles to Al Qaeda.* New York: Back Bay Books, 2006.

Levinson, Mark. "The Economic Collapse." *Dissent* (University of Pennsylvania Press), 2009: 61-66.

Lichetenwald, Terrance G., Mara H. Steinhour, and Frank S. Perri. "A Maritime Threat Assessment of Sea Based Criminal Organizations and Terrorist Operations." *Homeland Security Affairs* 8, no. 13 (August 2012): 1-24.

Lind, Wiliam S., Keith Nightengale, John F. Schmitt, Joseph W. Sutton, and Gary I. Wilson. "The Changing Face of War: Into the Fourth Generation." In *Global Insurgency and the Future of Armed Conflict*, edited by Terry Terriff, Karp, Aaron and Regina Karp, 13-20. New York: Routledge, 2008.

Lung, HaHa. *Assassin! The Deadly Art of the Cult of the Assassins*. New York: Citadel Press, 1997.

Lung, Haha. *Mind Control: The Ancient Art of Psychological Warfare*. New York: Citadel Press, 2006.

Mabon, Simon. "The Battle for Bahrain: Iranian-Saudi Rivalry." *Middle East Policy* 19, no. 2 (2012): 84-97.

Machiavelli, Niccolo. *The Prince*. Translated by Luigi Ricci. London: Grant Richards, 1903.

Machine, Garret. *Israeli Security Warrior Training*. Boulder: Paladin Press, 2011.

Magee, Aden C. "Counterintelligence in Irregular Warfare: A Void in the Full-Spectrum Joint Force Capability." *American Intelligence Journal*, Winter 2009: 54-60.

Manwaring, Max G. *A "New" Dynamic in the Western Hemisphere Security Environment: The Mexican Zetas and Other Private Armies*. Security Study, Carlisle: Strategic Studies Institute, 2009.

Manwaring, Max G. *State and Nonstate Associated Gangs: Credible "Midwives of New Social Orders"*. Strategic Study, Carlisle: Strategic Studies Institute, 2009.

Marcella, Gabriel. *War without Borders: The Colombia-Ecuador Crisis of 2008*. Strategic Study, Carlisle, PA: Strategic Studies Institute, 2008.

Marighella, Carlos. *Mini-Manual of the Urban Guerrilla*.

Marks, Thomas A. "A Model Counterinsurgency: Uribe's Colombia (2002-2006) vs FARC." *Military Review*, March-April 2007: 41-56.

Martines, Larry. "Mexican Crime Cartels." *Journal of Counterterrorism & Homeland Security International* 18, no. 1 (2012): 36-40.

May, Timothy. *THE MONGOL ART OF WAR: Chinggis Khan and the Mongol Military System*. Book Club. Yardley, PA: Westholme Publishing, 2007.

McLaughlin, Abraham. *A matter of ethics for cloak-and-dagger set*. 5 October 2001. http://www.csmonitor.com/2001/1005/p2s1-usju.html (accessed July 23, 2010).

McMains, Michael J, and Wayman C. Mullins. *Crisis Negotiations: Managing Critical Incidents and Hostage Situations in Law Enforcement and Corrections.* 4th. New Providence, NJ: Matthew Bender & Company, 2010.

McNicholas, Michael. *Maritime Security: An Introduction.* Burlington, MA: Elsevier, 2008.

McRaven, William H. *SPEC OPS: Case Studies in Special Operations Warfare: Theory and Practice.* New York: Ballantine Books, 1996.

Melton, H. Keith, and Robert Wallace. *The Official C.I.A. Manual of Trickery and Deception.* New York: William Morrow, 2009.

Mendell, Ronald L. *The Quiet Threat: Fighting Industrial Espionage in America.* Second. Springfield, IL: Charles C. Thomas Publisher, 2011.

Merari, Ariel. "The readiness to kill and die: Suicidal terrorism in the Middle East." In *Origins of Terrorism: Psychologies, Ideologies, Theologies, States of Mind,* by Walter Reich, 192-207. Washington: Woodrow Wilson Center Press, 1998.

Miller, Colin R. *Electromagnetic Pulse Threats in 2010.* Threat Analysis, Maxwell AFB: Center for Strategy and Technology, Air War College/Air University, 2005.

Milton-Edwards, Beverley. *Contemporary Politics in the Middle East.* Second Edition. Cambridge: Polity, 2006.

Minieri, Michael W. *Protecting Corporate Secrets: A Brief Primer on Contemporary Practices in Information Security.* White Paper, Reston: Kroll Schiff & Associates, 2004.

Morris, Benny. *Israel's Border Wars 1949-1956.* New York: Oxford University Press, Inc., 1997.

Murphy, Martin, N. *Small Boats, Weak States, Dirty Money: Piracy and Maritime Terrorism in the Modern World.* New York: Columbia University Press, 2010.

Musashi, Miyamoto. "The Book of Five Rings." 1645.

Nasheri, Hedieh. *Economic Espionage and Industrial Spying.* New York: Cambridge University Press, 2005.

Nutt, Steven, and Josh Lyons. *Virtual Worlds and Terrorist Attack Planning*. Shawnee, OK: Urban Warfare Analysis Center, 2008.

Oatman, Robert L. *Executive Protection: New Solutions for a New Era*. Arnold, Maryland: Noble House, 2006.

O'Neill, Bard E. *Armed Struggle in Palestine: A Political-Military Analysis*. Boulder: Westview Press, 1978.

Paladin Press. *Handbook for Volunteers of the Irish Republican Army*. Boulder, CO: Paladin Press, 1985.

—. *KGB Alpha Team Training Manual: How the Soviets Trained for Personal Combat, Assassination, and Subversion*. Boulder: Paladin Press, 1993.

Pastor, Robert A. *A Century's Journey: How the Great Powers Shape the World*. New York: Basic Books, 1999.

Pelton, Robert Young. *Licensed to Kill: Hired Guns in the War on Terror*. New York: Three Rivers Press, 2007.

Peters, Ralph. "Killing with Kindness: Political correctness infiltrates the Army." *Armed Forces Journal*, December 2006: 28-32.

—. "When Muslim armies won: Lessons from yesteryears's jihadi victories." *Armed Forces Journal*, September 2007: 38-41,47.

Phalen, D.J. "Protecting Those Who Save Lives." *The Journal of Counterterrorism & Homeland Security International* 17, no. 2 (2011): 24-26.

Poole, H. John. *Dragon Days: Time for "Unconventional" Tactics*. Emerald Isle, NC: Posterity Press, 2007.

—. *Global Warrior: Averting WWIII*. Emerald Isle, NC: Posterity Press, 2011.

—. *Militant Tricks: Battlefield Ruses of the Islamic Insurgent*. Emerald Isle, North Carolina: Posterity Press, 2005.

—. *Tactics of the Crescent Moon: Militant Muslim Combat Methods*. Emerald Isle, North Carolina: Posterity Press, 2004.

—. *Tequila Junction: 4th-Generation Counterinsurgency*. Emerald Isle, NC: Posterity Press, 2008.

—. *The Tiger's Way: A U.S. Private's Best Chance for Survival.* Emerald Isle, NC: Posterity Press, 2003.

Povlock, Paul A. "A Guerrilla War At Sea: The Sri Lankan Civil War." *Small Wars Journal.* Small Wars Foundation, 9 September 2011.

Powers Jr., James F. *Filling Special Operations Gaps with Civilian Expertise.* JSOU Report 07-1, Hurlburt Field: Joint Special Operations University, 2006.

Rabinovich, Abraham. *The Yom Kippur War: The Epic Encounter that Transformed the Middle East.* New York: Schocken, 2004.

Rambaud, Alfred. *History of Russia: From the Earliest Times to 1877.* Vol. II. New York: John B. Alden, 1886.

Randal, Jonathan. *Osama: The Making of a Terrorist.* New York: Vintage Books, 2004.

Randall, Albert B. "State-Building and the Double-Edged Sword of Religion." In *Stability Operations and State-Building: Continuities and Contingencies*, by Greg Kaufmann, 33-58. Carlisle, PA: Strategic Studies Institute, 2008.

Rashid, Ahmed. *Taliban: Militant Islam, Oil and Fundamentalism in Central Asia.* Second. New Haven, CT: Yale University Press, 2010.

Rassler, Don, and Vahid Brown. *The Haqqani Nexis and the Evolution of al-Qa'ida.* U.S. Army Harmony Program, United States Military Academy, West Point: The Combating Terrorism Center at West Point, 2011.

Ratner, Steven R. "Predator and Prey: Seizing and Killing Suspected Terrorists Abroad." *The Journal of Political Philosophy* 15, no. 3 (2007): 251-275.

Directed by Pierre Rehov. Produced by Pierre Rehov. 2006.

Reisman, W. Michael, and Chris T. Antoniou. *The Laws of War: A comprehensive collection of primary documents on international laws governing armed conflict.* New York: Random House, 1994.

Richelson, Jeffrey T. *A Century of Spies: Intelligence in the twentieth century.* New York: Oxford University Press, 1995.

Rooney, David. *Guerrilla: Insurgents, patriots, and terrorists from Sun Tzu to Bin Laden.* London: Brassey's, 2004.

Ross, John F. *War on the Run: The Epic Story of Robert Rogers and the Conquest of America's First Frontier.* New York: Bantam Books, 2009.

Rourke, John T., and Mark A. Boyer. *International Politics on the World Stage.* 7th Edition. New York: McGraw-Hill, 2008.

Sanchez, W. Alejandro. "Russia and Latin America at the Dawn of the Twenty-First Century." *Journal of Transatlantic Studies* 8, no. 4 (December 2010): 362-384.

Sawyer, Ralph D., trans. *The Seven Military Classics of Ancient China.* Boulder: Westview Press, 1993.

Schroen, Gary C. *First In: An Isider's Account of How the CIA Spearheaded the War on Terror in Afghanistan.* New York: Ballantine Books, 2007.

Seddiq, Ramin. *Border Disputes On The Arabian Peninsula.* Policy Watch #525, Washington: The Washington Institute for Near East Policy, 2001.

Shulsky, Abram N., and Gary J. Schmitt. *Silent Warfare: Understanding the World of Intelligence.* Third Edition. Washington: Potomac Books, 2002.

Shultz Jr., Richard H. "Showstoppers: Nine Reasons Why We Never Sent Our Special Operations Forces after al Qaeda before 9/11." In *Terrorism and Counterterrorism: Understanding the New Security Environment: Readings and Interpretations,* by Russell D., Sawyer, Reid L. Howard, 518-530. Dubuque, IA: McGraw-Hill, 2006.

Silinsky, Mark. "A Briefing Yet to Be Delivered: Islamism and the U.S. Defense Intelligence Community." *American Intelligence Journal* 28, no. 1 (2010): 160-163.

Sinno, Abdulkader H. *Organizations at War in Afghanistan and Beyond.* Ithaca, NY: Cornell University Press, 2008.

Sloan, Stephen, and Robert J. Bunker. *Red Teams and Counterterrorism Training.* Norman, OK: University of Oklahoma Press, 2011.

Smith, Eugene B. "The New Condottieri and U.S. Policy: The Privatization of Conflict and its Implications." *Parameters,* Winter 2003: 104-119.

Smith, Jim. *A Law Enforcement and Security Officers' Guide to Responding to Bomb Threats.* Second. Springfield, IL: Charles C. Thomas, 2009.

Sockut, Eugene. *Secrets of Street Survival -- Israeli Style: Staying alive in a Civilian War Zone*. Boulder: Paladin Press, 1995.

Spalding, Robert. *Drug Subs: The Worldwide Invasion by the Narco-Submarine Fleet*. Signal Mountain, TN: Spalding Publishing, 2010.

Spencer, Robert. *The Truth about Muhammad: Founder of the World's Most Intolerant Religion*. Washington: Regnery Publishing, 2006.

Sperry, Paul. *Infiltration: How Muslim Spies and Subversives have Penetrated Washington*. Nashville: Nelson Current, 2005.

Spicer, Mark. "Mexican Drug Cartels: The Growing Threat of the Sniper Attack." *Journal of Counterterrorism & Homeland Security International* 16, no. 4 (2011): 48-50.

Spulak Jr., Robert G. *A Theory of Special Operations: The Origin, Qualities, and Use of SOF*. JSOU Report 07-7, Hurlburt Field: Joint Special Operations University, 2007.

Steele, Robert D. *Human Intelligence: All Humans, All Minds, All the Time*. Carlisle, PA: Strategic Studies Institute, 2010.

Stojkovic, Stan, David Kalinich, and John Klofas. *Criminal Justice Organizations: Administration and Management*. Fifth Edition. Belmont, CA: Wadsworth, 2012.

Sullivan, John P., and Adam Elkus. "Narco-Armor in Mexico." *Small Wars Journal*, July 2011.

Summers Jr, Harry G. *On Strategy: A Critical Analysis of the Vietnam War*. New York: Presidio Press, 1982.

Swanson, Scott. "Viral Targeting of the IED Social Network System." *Small Wars Journal*, May 2007: 2-16.

Taber, Robert. *War of the Flea: The Classic Study of Guerrilla Warfare*. Washington: Potomac Books, 2002.

Tatar, Bradley. "Emergence of Nationalist Identity in Armed Insurrections: A Comparison of Iraq and Nicaragua." *Anthropological Quarterly*, 2005: 179-195.

Terrill, W. Andrew. *The Saudi-Iranian Rivalry and the Future of Middle East Security*. Carlisle, PA: Strategic Studies Institute, 2011.

Thomas, Evan. *The Very Best Men: The Daring Early Years of the CIA*. New York: Simon & Schuster, 2006.

Thomas, Timothy L. "Russian Tactical Lessons Learned Fighting Chechen Separatists." *Journal of Slavic Military Studies*, 2005: 731-766.

Thornton, Rod. *Organizational Change in the Russian Airborne Forces: The Lessons of the Georgian Conflict*. Carlisle, PA: Strategic Studies Institute, 2011.

Thurman, James T. *Practical Bomb Scene Investigation*. Boca Raton, FL: CRC Press, 2006.

Timmerman, Kenneth R. *Countdown to Crisis: The Coming Nuclear Showdown with Iran*. New York: Three Rivers Press, 2006.

Tripp, Charles. *A History of Iraq*. New York: Cambridge University Press, 2007.

Tse-tung, Mao. *On Guerrilla Warfare*. New York: Classic House Books, 2009.

Tucker, David. "Fighting Barbarians." *Parameters*, Summer 1998: 69-79.

Tucker, Johnathan B. *War of Nerves: Chemical Warfare from World War I to Al-Qaeda*. New York: Pantheon, 2006.

Turbiville Jr., Graham H. *Guerrilla Counterintelligence: Insurgent Approaches to Neutralizing Adversary Intelligence Operations*. JSOU Report 09-1, Hurlburt Field, FL: Joint Special Operations University, 2009.

Turbiville Jr., Graham H. *Hunting Leadership Targets in Counterinsurgency and Counterterrorist Operations: Selected Perspectives and Experiences*. JSOU Report 07-6, Hurlbert Field: Joint Special Operations University, 2007.

U.S. Army Training and Doctrine Command. *A Military Guide to Terrorism in the Twenty-First Century*. Army Handbook, Fort Leavenworth: Deputy Chief of Staff for Intelligence, 2003.

Ulrichsen, Kristian Coates. "Internal and External Security in the Arab Gulf States." *Middle East Policy* XVI, no. 2 (Summer 2009): 39-58.

United States Army. *FMI 3-34.119 Improvised Explosive Device Defeat*. Fort Leonard Wood: Department of the Army, 2005.

United States Catholic Conference, Inc. *Catechism of the Catholic Church.* New York: Doubleday, 1994.

United States Department of Homeland Security. *Terrorist Weaponization of Fire: Improvised Incendiary Devices (IID) and Arson.* Unclassified/For Official Use Only, Office of Intelligence, Transportation Security Administration, Washington: U.S. Government, 2008.

United States Department of the Army. *FM 31-21 Guerrilla Warfare and Special Forces Operations.* Field Manual, Washington: U.S. War Office, 1961.

United States Marine Corps. *FRONT-LINE INTELLIGENCE.* Field Manual FMFRP 12-16, Washington: Department of the Navy, 1988.

Vacca, John R. *Computer Forensics: Computer Crime Scene Investigation.* Hingham, MA: Charles River Media, Inc., 2002.

Velocity, Max. *Rapid Fire! Tactics for High Threat, Protection and Combat Operations.* Lexington, KY: Max Velocity, 2012.

Venter, Al J. *Allah's Bomb: The Islamic Quest for Nuclear Weapons.* Guilford, CT: The Lyons Press, 2007.

Waisberg, Tatiana. "The Colombia-Ecuador Armed Crisis of March 2008: The Practice of Targeted Killing and Incursions against Non-State Actors Harbored at Terrorist Safe Havens in a Third Party State." *Studies in Conflict & Terrorism* 32 (2009): 476-488.

Watkins, Lance J. *Self-propelled Semi-submersibles: The Next Great Threat to Regional Security and Stability.* Thesis, Monterey: Naval Post-Graduate School, 2011.

Waugh, Billy, and Tim Keown. *Hunting the Jackal.* New York: Avon Books, 2004.

West, John. *Fry the Brain: The Art of Urban Sniping and its Role in Modern Guerrilla Warfare.* Countryside, VA: SSI, 2008.

Wilkinson, Paul. *Terrorism & the Liberal State.* Second Edition. New York: New York University Press, 1986.

Williams, Phil. *Criminals, Militias, and Insurgents: Organized Crime in Iraq.* Carlisle, PA: Strategic Studies Institute, 2009.

Williams, Phil. "Transnational Criminal Networks." In *Networks and Netwars: The Future of Terror, Crime, and Militancy*, edited by John Arquilla and David Ronfeldt, 61-97. Santa Monica, California: RAND Corporation, 2001.

Williams, Phil, and Vanda Felbab-Brown. *Drug Trafficking, Violence, and Instability*. Carlisle, PA: Strategic Studies Institute, 2012.

Wilson, Brian. "Submersibles and Transnational Criminal Organizations." *Ocean and Coastal Law Journal*, 2011: 35-63.

Wimberley, Scott. *Special Forces Guerrilla Warfare Manual*. Boulder: Paladin Press, 1997.

Zuhur, Sherifa. *HAMAS and ISRAEL: Conflicting Strategies of Group-Based Politics*. Carlisle, PA: Strategic Studies Institute, 2008.

ABOUT THE AUTHOR

R.J. Godlewski (GOD LESS KEY) is the manager of Tactical Extractions, LLC., a threat resolution services company and the owner of several tactical security and counterterrorism businesses located throughout the United States. He is a graduate of American Military University, holding an M.A. in Military Studies, Asymmetrical Warfare concentration and a B.A. in Intelligence Studies, Terrorism Studies concentration, both earned with academic honors. He further holds graduate and undergraduate certificates in Security Management and Explosive Ordnance Disposal, respectively. Mr. Godlewski is a veteran of both the U.S. Navy and U.S. Navy Reserve.

www.Ingramcontent.com/pod-product-compliance
Lightning Source LLC
Chambersburg PA
CBHW020520290526
45786CB00002B/695